Endorsements

This is brilliant, amazingly concise yet incredibly detailed. It gives the facts but goes beyond – it teaches. John has successfully gathered hundreds of images that are easily assimilated by the reader. *Annette Miller - Missionary to India.*

John's passion for the Word of God has culminated in a commentary that is rich in understanding that will inspire the reader to apply the unique insights to their lives. *Alan Matson – Pastor.*

John relates his wealth of insight in the Bible and natural science to the reader in easily understood terms that are compact, dense and reader-friendly. I will turn to this valuable tool frequently. *Tony Hollick – Educator.*

For always selflessly dispensed wisdom and warmth and listening with under-standing. You've encouraged and guided with patience and care, and given so much of yourself. Its in salutation of your being a reformer and builder not only of (our company) but also of our character that we as students declare you as the greatest teacher, for in your footsteps we shall follow with pride. *Staff of Company in India on departing as Managing Director.*

A Layman's Commentary

Volume 2

Books
of
History

Joshua, Judges, Ruth 1 and 2 Samuel, 1 and 2 Kings,
1 and 2 Chronicles Ezra, Nehemiah, Esther

John Devine M Eng Sc

BALBOA.
PRESS
A DIVISION OF HAY HOUSE

Balboa Press books may be ordered through booksellers or by contacting:

Balboa Press
A Division of Hay House
1663 Liberty Drive
Bloomington, IN 47403
www.balboapress.com.au
1-(877) 407-4847

ISBN: 978-1-4525-1250-1 (sc)
ISBN: 978-1-4525-1251-8 (e)

Printed in the United States of America

Balboa Press rev. date: 12/11/2013

CONTENTS

Books of History

Twelve Books record the history of Israel as a nation – the rise and the fall. Nine cover the period from the entry into the Promised Land through the rule of judges and the line of kings to the exile in Babylon from 1406 to 586 BC a duration of some 820 years. The highlight was the reign of David the great king of Israel and the promise of God to establish through Jesus an everlasting kingdom for all nations. *The LORD God will give him the throne of his father David – his kingdom will never end Lk 1:32,33.*

The last three Books record the return of a remnant from the exile.

Joshua – The LORD is my Salvation

Introduction – The people of Israel had been prepared by bondage in Egypt over some 150 years and training in the wilderness for forty years. They had the instructions from God for building the new nation and were now set to enter the Promised Land of Canaan.

Joshua was born in slavery. At the time of the Exodus he was age 40 and led the Israelites in their first battle against Amalek 14:7: Ex 17:13. As aide to Moses he went onto Mt Sinai with him to receive the Ten Commandments Ex 24:13. After commissioning of the Tabernacle he accompanied Moses in the encounters with God and lingered in the Presence Ex 33:11.

A leader of the tribe of Ephraim Num 13:8; 14:6-9 he was one of the twelve spies sent to explore the new land and with Caleb brought back a positive report. These were the only two granted entry into the new land Num 14:30.

At 80 years of age he was appointed by God to succeed Moses to lead the people in the conquest of Canaan Num 27:18. He was a man in whom the Spirit of God dwelt Nu 27:18; Deu 34:9.

Author – Joshua, who became successor to Moses.

Period – Covers the entry, conquest and occupation of Canaan during the last thirty years of Joshua's life from around 1406 to 1376 BC.

The 'Israel' Stele from Egypt declaring the victory of Pharaoh Merneptah 1213-1203 BC, aging son of Ramses II over the inhabitants of Canaan in the 13th century identifies Israel as one of the defeated nations and confirms them as having been settled there at that time.

Theme - Conquest of the Promised Land The Book of Joshua is a high point in the history of Israel. Under his leadership the people were faithful and saw God's promise to Abraham some 500 years earlier fulfilled Gen 12:1. They had risen from a small nomadic family under Abraham to become a nation possessing the Promised Land.

The record is one of success as Joshua faithfully motivated the people to be true to the conditions of the Covenant established by God with Moses and he led them to enter their inheritance.

This Book of the Law Joshua left the people with a warning that their continued success would depend on their commitment to God and his ways 1:8,9. This is true today for the personal life of the believer, for society and for the nation. When we compromise our values, standards and beliefs we suffer.

Remove the offense The judgment on the inhabitants of Canaan was due to their evil practices Lev 18:21-23; Deu 12:29-32. God sets the standard in the heart and gives opportunity to repent but his justice is sure. Israel was warned that they would experience the same judgment if they failed to honor God 23:11-13; Gen 15:16; Nu 33:50-56.

THE FIRST INSTRUCTIONS TO JOSHUA

1:1 The LORD said to Joshua When Israel received the Covenant on Mt Sinai they became a Theocracy - they acknowledged God as their King. The leader acted on behalf of God. This demonstrated God's intention for involvement with his people. Moses fulfilled the role of leader and Joshua now took his place. He received his first instructions from the King.

1:2,3 I will give you every place where you set your foot Joshua was given command of Israel to lead them to conquer the land promised to Abraham and his descendants Gen 15:7. We are to extend the kingdom of God by witnessing for Jesus, our King. God promises to lead us and give us victory Mt 28:18-20.

1:4 The extent of the land The land possessed under Joshua extended from Beersheba in the Negeb wilderness in the south to Dan in the north bordering on Damascus and Mt Hebron 1Sam 3:20. It stretched from the shore of the Mediterranean Sea across the Jordan River to the Arabian Desert in the east Gen 15:18-21. It was extended under David and Solomon to the Persian Gulf in the south and to the Euphrates River in the north 2Chr 9:26.

1:5-7 I will never leave you nor forsake you Moses was dead - Joshua now faced the walled city of Jericho and the land beyond. Obedience and courage were required for success - including faith in God's promises. God's promise to be with Joshua is ours as well through Jesus Mt 28:20.

GUIDELINES FOR LIFE

1:8,9 Importance of God's Word The Book of the Law as compiled by Moses was the guide for the new nation of Israel Deu 31:24-26 (Genesis to Deuteronomy). The Bible including the Book of the Law is the source of guidance and power for the believer's life now - personally and as a nation.

Joshua was a military commander - yet the basis for successful living is the same for all walks of life. We are told to **read God's Word daily and apply it, to memorize it and meditate on it.** We are to fashion our lives on it – if *you remain in me and my words remain in you, ask whatever you wish and it will be given to you Jn 15:7*

• ***Do not let this Book of the Law depart from your mouth*** This means we should not only read it regularly but study it to see how to apply it in our daily living. God speaks to us through his Word. As he inspired the writers and people of old he will use it to teach, rebuke, correct and train us so that we also will be ready for every good work 2Tim 3:16

• ***meditate on it day and night*** We can only meditate on God's Word as we read it regularly and commit it to memory. The Holy Spirit then reminds us of God's promises. He also brings us new and fresh understanding

• ***so that you may be careful to do everything written in it*** The purpose of reading and studying the Word is not just to become knowledgeable but to apply God's instructions in our lives. It is by appropriating God's promises that we obtain victory in our personal lives and in our service.

• **Then *you will be prosperous and successful*** *v8* Success in all areas of life comes from commitment to God and his Word. *Seek first the kingdom of God and his righteousness and all these things will be given to you Mt 6:33.* This means all the things we need to live as well as the provision and power to serve him in the kingdom

• ***Have I not commanded you? Be strong and courageous*** *v9* It is important to come to an understanding with the LORD as to what he wants you to do. Many set out on a task or ministry without a firm conviction about their calling. It is only when we are fully convinced of our task that we can persevere through all situations and achieve our goal 2Cor 4:16-18; Heb 10:39

• ***Do not be terrified or discouraged*** There is no need for apprehension or concern when you know that the LORD your God will be with you wherever you go v9; Is 43:1-7. We have the same promise from Jesus that removes anxiety as we learn to live for him – *do not worry about your life – your heavenly Father knows that you need them Mt 6:23,32*

1:10-18 Joshua gave God's commands to the people through the officials and they embraced them enthusiastically. Those who had received their inheritance on the east of the Jordan were required to continue to help conquer the land Nu 32:1-42.

ENTERING THE PROMISED LAND
The Fertile Crescent - a region of rich agricultural land stretching in an arc from Egypt to the Persian Gulf including the great rivers of the Nile, Jordan, Tigris and Euphrates - called the birthplace of civilization, especially Mesopotamia, dating back to 3,000 BC. Canaan was the trade route between Egypt and the great northern nations of Assyria and Babylon when Israel took possession of it. The people displaced by Joshua are listed 3:10; 24:11 - and those who remained to test the people Jud 3:1-4.

2:1-24 **Exploring the Land** Jericho was a major city defending the eastern border of Canaan - protected by the Jordan Valley in the north and the Dead Sea in the south. Two spies were sent out secretly to explore the land and the defenses of the city. Recall the failure of the previous spies Nu 14:1-4.

They entered the house of Rahab, an inn-keeper located on the city wall v2. She told of the fear that had swept the land v11.

Rahab protected the spies and sought protection from the coming attack which the spies granted v12.

The spies gave a good report – *The LORD has surely given the whole land into our hands v24.* These spies saw through the eyes of faith Nu 13:30; 14:6-9. This conviction comes when you are sure of your calling **Crossing the Jordan River – amazing things!**

3:1-4 They were now camped at Shittim on the plains of Moab near Mt Nebo, east of the Jordan River from Jericho Num 33:49.

3:5 **Consecrate yourselves** They were required to commit wholeheartedly for the LORD would do amazing things. We take on great responsibility when we go in God's name - we must honor God with our thoughts, words and actions Lk 10:27.

3:6-17 **The priests carried the Ark** into the river and the water was cut off so the people could cross on dry land. This was a further test of the faith and obedience of the new generation of people. As with all tests of faith it will be further confirmation of the LORD's blessing if we are faithful.

4:1-24 **Twelve stones** were taken from the river as a memorial of the crossing to remind future generations. The priests brought the Ark out of the river and the water returned - representing separation from the past. **Gilgal** The people made camp several km from the Jordan and north from Jericho. This was to be their base for the campaigns into Canaan.

5:1-9 **Circumcision** The miracle of the river crossing increased the fear of the Canaanites for the people of Israel. The Covenant condition of circumcision instituted with Abraham was confirmed by the people Gen 17:11.

5:10-12 **They celebrated the Passover** on the evening of the fourteenth day of the first month (Nisan) one year after leaving Egypt, to the day Ex 12:1 – the next day the manna stopped appearing and they ate of the fruit of the Promised Land v11.

The Commander of the LORD's Army

5:13-15 As commander of the army of the LORD I have come v14. Joshua was ready to lead the attack against Jericho. As he meditated on the course of action he had an encounter with the LORD to remind him that the battle was not his but the LORD's.

We need to wait on the LORD as we undertake his work by drawing aside to pursue him. When we know his Presence we will receive direction and power.

We serve in the knowledge that it is not our battle, but the LORD's; not our power, but the LORD's; not our glory, but the LORD's. *Not by might nor by power, but by my Spirit, says the LORD Almighty Zec 4:6.*

The LORD comes not as helper or assistant but as Commander! This knowledge is both humbling and empowering as we serve under the same Commander!

When Joshua sought instruction he was directed to worship v15.

Joshua's Preparation We can see what makes a great leader -

• He had a personal relationship with God that he developed by spending time in his presence Ex 24:13; 33:11, Nu 27:18-23

• He had experienced deliverance from bondage in Egypt

• He knew the hand of the LORD in battle and the power of prayer Ex 17:11. He saw the impact and consequences of negative attitude Nu 13:31

• He was confident that God would fulfill his promises 23:14

• He gave total commitment to the task and to the LORD.

THE CENTRAL CAMPAIGN

The land consisted of a loose confederacy of city states and nations. The LORD led Joshua to defeat the central cities of Canaan driving a wedge between the kings of the north and south. This provided time to go to Shechem to renew the Covenant. During this period they learned valuable lessons about obedience and the importance of inquiring of the LORD.

The Fall of Jericho

6:1-25 **Jericho under siege** God gave Joshua instructions for the battle v3. They marched openly around the city with the Ark each day for six days with the priests blowing trumpets. On the seventh day they circled the city seven times and gave a shout – *the LORD has given you the city v16* - the walls collapsed and they captured Jericho. This was a further test of faith against natural circumstances Heb 11:30.

The city and all that is in it is devoted to the LORD v17 Jericho was the first city to be taken in the Promised Land. The LORD commanded that everything in it be consecrated to him. Israel was used to bring judgment on the nations of Canaan for their idolatry and corrupt ways. Every idol and person had to be destroyed so that Israel would not be led to follow the evil practices. Israel was to be *a people holy to the LORD Deu 7:1-6.* God's judgment on the evil practices of the inhabitants of Canaan was predicted Gen 15:16.

6:25 **An Example of Grace and Faith** Rahab and her household were spared because of her faith in protecting the spies. She was one of two women, with Ruth, included in the lineage of Jesus Mt 1:5. She is listed with the hero's of faith Heb 11:31 and as righteous because of her act of faith Jas 2:25. This shows the mercy of God and his willingness to include in his kingdom anyone who turns to him in faith 2Pet 3:9. The scarlet cord reminds us of the Passover and the blood of Christ by which we are saved 2:18.

An Unfaithful Act – Achan's sin

7:1-26 **Obedience** The LORD required everything in Jericho to be consecrated – this was a further test of faith. One of the soldiers took some of the valuable items and hid them for himself. As a result all the people were held to account.

Joshua sent a small force against the next city of Ai - perhaps he was self-confident with success - he did not inquire of the LORD v2. This confirms the importance of our time each day with God and the need to check issues in his Presence. It seemed a small task but the contingent was routed v4.

Joshua went to the LORD and was told that obedience to God's commands was required v7. So often we inquire after the event!

Then the LORD turned from his fierce anger v26. We see the consequences of coveting - the desire to go against what we know to be right v21. Judgment was executed on Achan and his family - they had been given warning and were complicit 6:16-19. Then Israel could go on with the campaign.

We must be obedient to God's Word. We are protected from God's judgment on sin by the death of Jesus in our place Jn 3:16.

Ai Captured – the campaign continued

8:1-29 Joshua was told to set an ambush – God uses our natural ability and at other times he performs miracles. In every case for the people of God they are amazing things! The people were permitted to take the plunder for themselves. If Achan had waited he would have prospered as God had promised v27.

The Covenant Renewed at Mt Ebal Deu 27:1-8

8:30-35 Moses had commanded the Covenant be renewed once they entered the Promised Land. They now had access to central Canaan so they moved north to Mt Ebal near Shechem, 45 km north of Jerusalem to build an altar to the LORD as written in the Book of the Law. Joshua copied on stones the words of the Law as given to Moses and the people assembled in two groups – one by Mt Ebal and one by Mt Gerizim. Joshua then read the Words of the Law for the people to hear.

9:1-27 **Deception by Gibeon** The success at Jericho brought the kings of Canaan together for council of war. The residents of Gibeon (a major city close to Ai) sent a delegation in disguise to gain peace with Israel. Israel again did not inquire of the LORD v14 and so were tricked into making a treaty. Joshua assigned the Gibeonites to servant duties. Again this event emphasizes the importance of prayer – to inquire of the LORD!

THE SOUTHERN CAMPAIGN – the Sun stood still

10:1-43 Five Amorite kings from the south joined forces to attack Israel at Gibeon v5. Joshua brought the army from their camp at Gilgal. After a 30 km night march they surprised the Amorites and defeated them - *the LORD threw them into confusion v10.* At the height of the battle the LORD extended the day at Joshua's request to allow Israel to complete the defeat. While the explanation of this event is uncertain it shows the extent to which God will intervene for the sake of his people and purposes. It is good to be in a position where you know that the battle is the LORD's v25.

The five kings were killed and the central city of Makkedah was taken v16. The remaining southern cities of Libnah, Lachish, Eglon, Hebron and Debir were conquered v29. This represented the whole territory explored by the twelve spies some forty years before – from Kadesh Barnea to Gibeon v40-43. The army then returned to the camp at Gilgal.

THE NORTHERN CAMPAIGN

11:1-23 The kings in the north formed a combined army and camped at Merom, north of the Sea of Galilee. Joshua defeated the army again by surprise. This gave Joshua control over the whole of Canaan v16. The land had rest from war v23.

12:1-24 The list of the thirty-one defeated kings in Canaan is given. The brevity of these two reports emphasizes the swiftness & decisiveness of the victory.

DIVISION OF THE LAND

13:1-33 A number of areas remained to be taken - they would cause temptation and corruption in the future.

East of Jordan had been assigned to the tribes of Ruben, Gad and the half tribe of Manassseh Nu 32:1.

14:1-5 **West of Jordan** was divided amongst the other nine and a half tribes by lot.

14:6-15 **Give me this Mountain** Caleb, of the tribe of Judah who with Joshua had given a positive report now requested Hebron, city of the Anakites as his possession - the specific area they had spied out 40 years before and which had caused the people's fear. Though Caleb was now 85 years old and the city had yet to be conquered he said *give me this hill country that the LORD promised me that day – the LORD helping me, I will drive them out v12*. Caleb followed the LORD wholeheartedly – may this be our confidence and aim! Nu 13:22,33.

15:1-63 **Allotment for Judah** - Jerusalem was finally taken Jud 1:8 but the Jebusites could not be dislodged until conquered by David 15:63; 2Sam 5:6-9.

16:1 to 17:18 **Allotment for Ephraim and Manasseh** – the sons of Joseph each received an inheritance representing Joseph because of their number. These two tribes replaced Levi in the numbering of the twelve tribes.

18:1-10 **The Tabernacle at Shiloh** 18:1; 1Sam 1:3.

Shiloh - this location 15 km north of Bethel and 30 km north of Jerusalem was chosen as the place of worship and the Tabernacle was set up there. For 250 years it would be the place for making major decisions until the Ark was surrendered to the Philistines in the days of Eli 1Sam 4:11.

18:11-28 **Allotment for Benjamin**

19:1-51 **Allotment for Simeon, Zebulun, Issachar, Asher, Naphtali and Dan.** Joshua received a special inheritance 19:49.

20:1-9 **Cities of Refuge** Six towns would allow security for accused people until proven guilty (presumption of innocence).

21:42 **Towns for the Levites** were allotted in each tribal area.

The Lord Gave Them Rest

21:43-45 This was fulfilment of God's promise to Abraham regarding possession of the Promised Land Gen 15:18-21.

22:1-34 The Tribes from east of Jordan returned home.

Joshua's Farewell

23:1-16 Joshua was 110 years old and following the campaign of five years Israel had known peace in the Promised Land for twenty-five years -

• *It was the LORD your God who fought for you v3* Remember that it is God who makes the difference in all we do and we should honor him

• *Be very strong; be careful to obey all that is written in the Book of the Law of Moses v6* Joshua made it clear that their success was due to their persistence, diligence and vigilance in reading and obeying God's Word. The same principle applies today in the believer's life

• *Not one of all the good promises the LORD your God gave you has failed. Every promise has been fulfilled v14.* We know that every promise of God applies today in Christ as we read and apply God's Word 2Cor 1:20.

The Covenant Affirmed at Shechem

Shechem – 15 km north of Shiloh was the place of Covenant 8:30 - the first place to be visited by Abraham Gen 12:6. It became capital of the northern kingdom of Israel until replaced by Samaria 885 BC 1Kin 12:25; 16:24.

24:1-13 They presented before God Joshua assembled all the tribes of Israel before God and called them to renew their commitment. He reviewed the history of the people from Abraham's call in Ur to the fulfilment of God's promise with their possession of the Promised Land Gen 15:18-20. We should renew our commitment regularly as we receive God's blessings and provision - health, peace, security and prosperity.

24:14 **Now fear the LORD and serve him with all faithfulness** We turn to God in times of trouble – we must commit to follow him in times of blessing as well. Faithfulness requires daily diligence to God's Word.

24:15-18 Choose for yourselves this day whom you will serve – but as for me and my household, we will serve the LORD v15 We must decide to make a personal choice today and every day that we will serve God.

24:19-27 You are not able to serve the LORD - He is a holy and jealous God v19 Joshua knew from past experience that the people would fail despite their profession v21. This is tragically chronicled in the remaining Books of History leading up to the loss of Israel's nationhood. God calls us to live separate from the world's standards and be devoted to him.

24:28-30 Joshua died at 110 years.

24:31-33 Israel served the LORD throughout the lifetime of Joshua and the elders who outlived him This confirms the need for godly leadership and a good succession plan Deu 31:14.

Judges

Introduction - While the Book of Joshua was a high point in the history of Israel as they entered the Promised Land so Judges was an extreme low point. Joshua showed that success is possible if we follow God's ways - Judges warns that failure is likely without God. It shows the weakness of human nature and the inability of mankind to save themselves without the presence of a God-anointed leader. For this reason people began to look for a Messiah, a Savior, One who would come from God and lead the people of the world in the right way. This need was fulfilled with the coming of Jesus.

Author – Events were recorded by local Levites at the time and compiled into a record during the time of Samuel.

Period – From Joshua's death 1376 BC to Eli 1148 BC over 228 years.

Theme – Prosperity and oppression The Theocratic system of priest and tribal 'family' leaders implemented by Moses and firmly established under Joshua was intended to lead Israel to peace and prosperity as they faithfully recognized God as King. Judges describes the failure of the people to follow the way of life set down by God in his Laws. The land was subdued under Joshua but the people did not completely drive out the inhabitants. Instead they conformed, integrated and intermarried. One can only contemplate the situation in the Middle East today. They did not remain faithful to their calling, adopting the idols, practices and standards of the world – in fact they became worse. They reverted to tribal locations. Twelve judges are mentioned. Eli and Samuel followed. Some of the time-spans may have been concurrent. The role of a judge is defined in Ex 18:13,15,22. As well as deciding matters of justice the judge was required to take leadership of the people.

There were successive cycles of prosperity and failure This long period of compromise and adopting the standards and practices of the world around them resulted in the progressive deterioration of Israel as a nation. The major message from the Book of Judges for today is that there will be continued conflict, economic hardship and oppression while ever unbridled human nature reigns. We look forward to the One who will reign in righteousness for eternity Is 9:6-7.

Ordinary Heroes The deliverers God raised up came from different walks of life with the one distinguishing quality – they were people of faith Heb 11. While we remember their weaknesses we must learn from their strengths – that God can use anyone who is committed to him in faith 5:2,9; Mt 17:20; Lk 1:38. We should also remember in the good times that it is God who provides all our needs Deu 8:18-20.

FAILURE TO SECURE THE LAND – missed opportunity

***1:1-36* After Joshua there was no successor** Joshua had made lightning raids and defeated the city kings of Canaan making the way open for the people to settle. Individual tribes were left to claim their inheritance and to drive out the local inhabitants.

They began by inquiring of the LORD as Moses and Joshua had before them. Judah succeeded in establishing their territory v2. They captured Jerusalem but failed to drive out the Jebusites who remained until David v8; 2Sam 5:6,7. The descendants of Joseph captured Bethel v22.

The remaining tribes had limited success. They were not faithful in their allegiance to God's Word. They compromised by allowing heathen people to live among them and influence them. They became self-centered and complacent in their way of life without giving God first place.

***1:20* Caleb's Success** This man of faith is an example to us – he obtained his inheritance because he followed the LORD his God wholeheartedly Jos 14:6-15.

***2:1* Angel of the LORD** After a period of disobedience the LORD withdrew his direct Presence leaving an angel to represent him - this had occurred before when the people had rebelled at Mt Sinai Ex 33:1-3.

***2:2-19* Pattern of the Book of Judges** Because the tribes did not completely conquer the land but accepted the presence of corrupt people and began to followed their ways they lost the protection provided through Joshua. Compromise always leads to thorns and snares v2,3. The people were oppressed by their foreign neighbors because they did not listen to God. Oppression is a sign of God's mercy as he seeks to gain our attention. He disciplines us because he is more interested in our character than our comfort.

The new generation who had not seen the things God had done knew about him but chose to ignore him v10.

A cycle developed with five stages -
- the people turned from God in the times of prosperity v11
- God sent persecution so that they might remember him v14
- they repented and called to the LORD to rescue them 3:9,15
- God intervened by raising up a judge to deliver them v16

- they experienced reform and peace for a period before returning to the evil ways v19.

This cycle is lived out in every generation Deu 28:1 to 30:20.

The sinful nature of mankind is apparent 2:11,17,19; 8:33-35; 10:6; 13:1.

2:20-23 **Again Israel failed to reach their potential** as the people of God. The remaining nations were used to test them in their allegiance. When we fail to move on in our commitment further testing comes. God must always bring us to an end of ourselves and our hopes before we will respond to the saving grace of God. The people failed to enter the 'rest of faith' under Joshua Heb 4:8. This rest is available to those who put their faith in Jesus Christ Heb 4:9-11.

3:1-6 **The nations left unconquered to test Israel** Canaanites, Hittites, Amorites, Perizzites, Hivites and Jebusites Gen 15:18-21. They intermarried with the local people and adopted their idols v6; Nu 33:50-55.

THE LORD RAISED UP JUDGES

After Joshua the tribes remained in isolated locations. The periods of oppression and deliverance are not in sequence. If we consider the claim by Jephthah that Israel had possessed Heshbon for 300 years his time would be around 1100 BC 11:26. Some of the campaigns were localized and some overlapped, particularly after Jephthah and around the time of Eli.

The dates following are based on this statement with some overlap, allowing 40 years for the elders who outlived Joshua.

Seven Specific Periods of Judgment are noted throughout the country. In every case God intervened to raise a leader 2:16.

3:7-11 **OTHNIEL** 1336 BC Judgment comes on those who choose to forget the LORD v7. Caleb's nephew delivered Israel when they were oppressed by Aram (Syria) in the north. Aram were Semitic migrants from beyond Mesopotamia Gen 10:22,23.

We can inspire others or be inspired – lead or be led v10.

The Spirit of the LORD came upon him The Spirit led specific leaders in the past 6:34; 11:29; 13:25; 14:6,19; 15:14. Now the Spirit is within all who believe to lead and empower them in service Acts 1:8.

3:12-30 **EHUD** 1296 BC They were attacked by Moab from the south east and were delivered by a man of courage - he made opportunity and took action – at great personal effort and risk he stepped out in faith and accomplished God's purpose.

***3:31* SHAMGAR** delivered Israel from the Philistines, the Sea People, who migrated from Cyprus and Crete around 1200 BC. They occupied five cities of the south coast Jos 13:2,3 and were Israel's major threat until subdued by David 2Sam 5:17-25.

***4:1-24* DEBORAH** 1216 BC The Canaanites of Hazor in the central north rose against them. Deborah, a prophetess led Israel at the time and motivated Barak to deliver them - she gave him a command from the LORD together with a plan v6. Barak was afraid - he required Deborah to sense God's presence. Yet he overcame his fears, stepped out in faith and experienced victory v15; Heb 11:32 - this is a pattern for us to follow.

5:1-31 **Deborah's Psalm of Praise** –

•   faith is only as strong as the knowledge on which it is based – as we grow in our relationship with God our faith is strengthened. Deborah was leader of the people because her faith was strong v2,3

•   she recognized it was God who gave them the victory v4,5

•   she knew that God uses the willing volunteer v9. God can do the impossible but he always chooses a person Jn 14:12

•   those who love the LORD will shine like the sun in the kingdom of their Father – both in this life and the life to come v31; Mt 5:16; 13:43.

***6:1-40* GIDEON** 1176 Midianites from the southeast wilderness, descendants of Abraham Gen 25:2, invaded Israel. The reason - *but you have not listened to me v10.*

•   again God chose one man - from among all Israel v11

•   Gideon was an ordinary person - hiding in a winepress

•   he met an ordinary angel - God usually speaks through a still small voice - not the thunder we might expect 1Kin 19:11-15

•   Gideon felt inadequate - a sign of being useful to God v15

•   the LORD called Gideon *you mighty warrior v12*

•   he was told *go in the strength you have* - God knows our potential

•   we need to see ourselves as God sees us - the victory does not depend on our ability but that the LORD is with us v13,14,16

•   Gideon was required to clean out his father's house v25 - we must deal with anything that stands between us and God

•   Gideon questioned God three times v 17,36-40

•   the LORD anointed Gideon for the task - with His Spirit v34

•   action starts with our perception of who God is and what he can do in us.

7:1-25 The Army is Too Large We may consider we are not sufficient - twice Gideon was told to reduce his numbers - those afraid, those not prepared. The 32,000 soldiers he raised were slimmed to 300 so that *Israel may not boast against me that her own strength has saved her v2.*

8:1-27 Gideon had trouble with the pride of the Israelites not included in the battle. Despite his victory he led the people to idol worship. Having torn down his family's idols he made a symbol of pride. He departed from the values he had learned.

8:28-35 Return to the old ways After Gideon's death the people forgot the cause of their hardship and the source of their salvation - *they did not remember the LORD their God v34.*

9:1-57 The Consequence of Evil Gideon's illegitimate son slaughtered his seventy half-brothers and took over leadership with disastrous results.

10:1-5 TOLA and JAIR ruled for a period.

10:6-18 Israel again did what they were told not to do and became subject to the Philistines from the south west and Ammonites in the east (descendents of Lot who lived on the far east of Jordan against the Arabian desert Gen 19:38. Moses drove them back from the Jordan and the area was settled by Gilead, descendant of Joseph's son Manasseh Nu 26:29,30.)

When the people came to acknowledge their rebellion and disobedience the LORD responded. This opportunity is available today to individuals, families and nations.

11:1-27 JEPHTHAH 1106 BC Jephthah of Gilead was an unlikely hero v1-3. He acted in faith that God would defend the people once they had repented 15:15,16. He knew his heritage and recalled God's provision in the past.

For 300 years Israel occupied Heshbon – occupied by Abraham and conquered by Moses Gen 13:18; Nu 21:25. Those who are faithful live under God's provision v26-29. If Moses captured Heshbon in 1407 BC Jephthah's time would be around 1106 BC.

11:28-33 Because of his confession of faith the Spirit of the LORD came on Jephthah and gave him victory over Ammon.

11:28-40 A foolish vow In arrogance he made a foolish, impulsive and unnecessary vow which was not of faith, based on the practices of the heathen nations v30,31; Mt 5:33-37. Our future is influenced by the words we speak Mt 12:36.

12:1-7 Unnecessary conflict with Ephraim west of Jordan.

12:8-15 **IBZAN, ELON and ABDON** also led Israel.

13:1-25 **SAMSON** delivered Israel from the Philistines. Raised up by God v3 with godly parents, he was a Nazirite, set apart to God Nu 6:2 – conditions applied v4,5. His commitment to the rule showed his devotion and the source of power as he responded to the stirring of the Spirit of the LORD v25.

14:1-11 **Samson was a capable leader** but careless in his lifestyle. He made a foolish marriage choice – a Philistine woman who was used by God v4. The incident with the lion demonstrated his potential strength v5.

14:12-20 **His riddle** has kingdom significance – those who receive the good news about Jesus share it with others; this requires commitment and brings joy v14; Rev 10:8-11. His anger began his action against the Philistines v19.

15:1-20 **Fire in the Fields** He took vengeance on the Philistines. To have the most impact he caught foxes, set them on fire and set them among the fields to destroy the food supply. This resulted in further suppression of the Philistines. We must find ways to get the fire of the Gospel into the fields.

16:1-31 **Compromise** He formed a relationship with Delilah, who caused his downfall when he betrayed his faith – he violated his vow. There are consequences to our actions and regret over emotional decisions. As Samson acknowledged his weakness, his strength returned and he was again used to bring about God's purpose. In a final act of faith he brought down the Temple of Dagon and killed many more Philistines gaining deliverance for his people v23,30. He led the people for forty years.

Samson is a classic example of one who betrays principle for desire which brings failure. Leaders must follow sound judgment and righteous principles rather than emotion and desire.

Deteriorating Conditions – Idolatry and Immorality

This period shows the depth to which the people of Israel had fallen. One can only wonder at the lofty position at Mt Sinai as God's treasured position with the Ten Commandments. Within a few generations they were motivated by self interest and lack of restraint. They had turned away from the Covenant conditions and followed the ways of the heathen people. Human nature needs constraint because of original sin - the tendency to chose wrong over what we know is right Pro 29:18. God's judgment is on those who refuse to acknowledge his ways Nu 33:50-56; Ps 14:1-3; Rom 3:10-20.

17:1-13 An Ephraimite made a shrine and idols, employing a Levite as priest, all contrary to the Word of God. Like so many this man thought he could adopt those parts of God's Word that suited him and so be pleasing to God.

18:1-31 People from Dan moved into the area, slaughtered the local inhabitants and stole the idols and the Levite. How the chosen people were fallen. They set up local worship rather than go to the Tabernacle at Shiloh v31.

19:1-21:24 In another incident a Levite traveling through Gibeah with his wife was shamefully mistreated by the locals resulting in civil war and the death of many Benjamite men 20:1. Special provision had to be made to find wives to maintain the tribal heritage 21:1. Most of the problems faced by society are as a result of rebellious human nature.

21:25 **Degradation of Israel** The concluding verse shows the sad state of Israel within years of the death of Joshua - *in those days Israel had no king; everyone did as he saw fit*. Compare this with - *Israel served the LORD throughout the lifetime of Joshua and the elders who outlived him Jos 24:31.*

Ruth

Introduction – After the disappointing record of the period of Judges the Book of Ruth outlines a story of the commitment of a foreign woman to the people of God. Ruth was from Moab and became great-grandmother of king David. She is one of two women (both foreigners) included in the genealogy of Jesus Mt 1:5; the other being Rahab who was the mother of Boaz.

Author – It may have been a family member, handed down to Samuel because of interest in the line of kings.

Period – Towards the end of the period of Judges 1200 BC.

Theme – God's Mercy and Grace This is a story of love and devotion as well as an important part of history. It demonstrates God's sovereignty and mercy in that even in the midst of failure *in all things God works for the good of those who love him who have been called according to his purpose Rom 8:28.*

The Kinsman-Redeemer The concept of Kinsman-Redeemer applies to the coming of Christ as our Kinsman-Redeemer. He is the one who redeems us from our sins Gal 4:4,5.

Salvation for all who believe - The inclusion of a Moabite in the royal line confirms that the Messiah would come to redeem not only his people Israel but all people Lk 1:68; 2:30-32.

A Sad Beginning – Misfortune for Ruth and Naomi in Moab

1:1-15 In the days when the judges ruled there was famine in the land. The famine was due to disobedience and rejection of God and was typical of the cycles experienced at that time Deu 28:15-19,45-48; Jud 2:10-14. Bethlehem means 'house of bread' – but there was no bread in the house because of the disobedience of the people. A family from Bethlehem moved to the foreign country of Moab descendants of Lot some 80 km south east of Jerusalem across the Jordan because of the famine. After some ten years the man and his two sons died v3,5.

Naomi, the woman and her two daughters-in-law were left without support. When Naomi decided to return to Bethlehem she encouraged the girls to return to their families. One daughter-in-law, Orpah returned, the other one, Ruth, chose to remain with Naomi and go back to Judah.

1:16-18 Your people will be my people and your God, my God. Ruth gave her allegiance to Naomi and the God of Israel.

1:19-22 The Almighty has brought misfortune upon me Naomi felt that she had gone away full, but the LORD had brought her back empty. We sometimes feel that hardship is the result of the disfavor of God. Often we cannot see God's purpose in the events in our lives but it is always there. Patience and perseverance produce maturity and blessing Jas 1:1-4.

A Happy Meeting – Ruth and Boaz

2:1-23 Boaz was a man of standing in Israel of the royal line of Judah and a relative of Naomi's deceased husband.

Ruth demonstrated her commitment to Naomi by working in the field v2. It was the custom in Israel to leave fallen grain for the unfortunate. Boaz, the owner of the field was attracted to Ruth. He saw she was diligent and inquired about her.

Boaz pronounced a blessing on Ruth *May the LORD repay you – under whose wings you have come to take refuge v12.*

The Kinsman-Redeemer

Naomi recognized that Boaz was a relative of the family and a potential kinsman-redeemer v20. This provision was included in the Law to protect widows and provide perpetuity of inheritance. It meant that in the event of a death the nearest relative had the right and responsibility to marry the widow, provide for her, raise children and develop the land Deu 25:5,7.

3:1-18 After a time Naomi advised Ruth to approach Boaz about his responsibility as kinsman-redeemer. *Spread the corner of your garment over me since you are a kinsman-redeemer v9* This act was a reminder of the custom and a request for him to provide for her. Boaz agreed to pursue his responsibility.

God's Purpose Revealed – a famous off-spring

4:1-10 It was necessary for Boaz to confront a closer relative to obtain the right to marry Ruth. This was given.

4:11-12 **May you have standing and be famous in Bethlehem through your offspring** – this was a prophetic statement as their great grandson became King David, faithful ruler of Israel, man after the heart of God and the forerunner of Jesus Christ who was born of Mary in Bethlehem Mt 1:5,6,16.

4:13-22 **Boaz and Ruth Married** They named their son Obed. The local women said to Naomi *may he become famous throughout Israel v14.*

1 Samuel – 'asked of God'

Introduction – The two Books of Samuel were originally one. Towards the end of the turbulent years of decline under the judges Samuel became the last of the **Judges of Israel** and brought about reform. However despite his faithful ministry the people demanded that a king be appointed over them - like the other nations! They would prefer to be ruled by a person than pursue a relationship with God.

It was the end of **Theocracy** where God was acknowledged as King and the beginning of **Monarchy** where a man was chosen as king. The Theocracy (from Moses to Samuel) lasted 396 years – the Monarchy (from Saul to the Exile) would last 464 years. The Monarchy required that **prophets** be raised to speak on behalf of God. Samuel was the first of the great prophets after Moses Acts 3:24. He was a **priest** and man of faith Heb 11:32.

United Kingdom – With the appointment of Saul as king 1050–1010 BC Israel became a United Kingdom for 120 years with the reigns of David 1010–970 BC and Solomon 970–930 BC. Israel developed under David to a position of security and power. David was recognized as a **prophet, priest and king** Acts 2:30; 2Sam 5:3; 6:17. These titles would apply to Jesus.

Author – Samuel 1Chr 29:29. It was the practice of leaders to record their significant acts 2Sam 8:16. The prophets, scribes and king's recorders kept the records after the death of Samuel.

Period – Some 140 years from Samuel's birth to David's death.

Theme – Transition from judge to king The change of leadership from judge to king indicated that the people were rejecting God as King 8:7. The period of Judges showed the failure of human leaders to make permanent change in the conduct of people and the need for a Messiah who would deliver mankind from the influence of sin Deu 18:15,18.

1Samuel Seven chapters record the life of Samuel, born around 1110 BC becoming judge after the death of Eli around 1080 BC. God appointed Saul as the first king who met the worldly standards the people were demanding and despite the anointing he failed. The remaining chapters describe the reign of Saul and his insane pursuit of David.

2Samuel Tells of the reign of David whom God appointed as a man after God's heart 1Sam 13:14. He became a great king leading Israel to prosperity. He ruled Judah from 1010 BC and all Israel from 1003 BC until 970 BC. His failures are recorded as well as the consequences. We can learn from the failures of Saul and the faithfulness and submissiveness of David who was the forerunner of Jesus the King of kings.

SUMMARY
The Birth and Ministry of Samuel 1:1 to 7:17
The End of Theocracy and Beginning of Monarchy 8:1-22
Saul Chosen as King 9:1 to 15:35
David Anointed as Future King 16:1 to 21:15
The Making of a King 22:1-5
The Failure of a King 22:6 to 31:13

The Birth and Dedication of Samuel
1:1-9 Elkanah was a faithful worshiper at the Tabernacle each year. His wife Hannah was childless. **Shiloh** was located 30 km north of Jerusalem. It was the site of the Tabernacle and the Ark of the Covenant since the days of Joshua when Israel settled the Promised Land Jos 18:1; 19:51. There were three annual feasts which men sought to attend Ex 23:14-17. Eli, of the family of Levites, was the aging priest serving at the Tabernacle
The LORD Almighty v3 – a compound name of God Is 6:1-3.
1:10-20 **An Answer to Prayer** While the family attended the feast at Shiloh Hannah prayed and made a vow – if the LORD gave her a son she would set him apart for the service of God (as a Nazirite Jud 13:5). She offered what she most desired v11. Her prayer was answered and she called her son Samuel – 'asked of the LORD'. Her bitterness of soul, much weeping and intercessory prayer resulted in the birth of the great prophet, priest and judge.
1:21-28 After he was weaned she presented Samuel at Shiloh to grow up in the service of the Tabernacle - she would not have foreseen his greatness.
2:1-11 **My heart rejoices in the LORD** Her prayer of thanksgiving shows the joy of trust. We also see the holiness of God who made all things, knows all things and exalts his anointed v2,9,10. Samuel grew and ministered before the LORD.

2:12-17 **The Failure of Eli** His sons acting as priests were wicked. They used their father's position to corrupt the duties of the priesthood. Some people reject God and his Word because of the failures of organized religion. This only confirms the weakness of human nature and the need for a Savior. We lose out when we jettison good because of evil.

2:18 Samuel was ministering before the LORD – as a boy!

2:19-25 The LORD was gracious to Hannah Because of her devotion and faithfulness in fulfilling her vow Hannah was blessed by God – with three sons and two daughters.

Eli rebuked his sons but they did not listen v22-25.

2:26 The boy Samuel continued to grow in stature and in favor with the LORD and with men – when we are faithful to God he gives us favor with others v30.

2:27-36 **Judgment on Eli's House** Because of the failure of the Levitical priesthood to teach the people Eli's family would be cut off. *I will raise up for myself a faithful priest – he will minister before my anointed one* – that priest was already growing, the boy Samuel. This prophecy was fulfilled with the anointing of David v35; 16:13 – ultimately leading to Jesus.

Samuel Learned to Hear from God

3:1-6 In those days the Word of the LORD was rare; there were not many visions When we do not read the Word of God on a regular basis we rarely hear from God. Samuel faithfully waited on God daily – his last task was to trim the candles in the Tabernacle.

The Lord called Samuel – when we wait on the LORD daily he speaks to us, guides and instructs us v4 - it requires discipline, dedication and patience – then response.

3:7-9 Samuel did not yet know the LORD; the Word of the LORD had not yet been revealed to him We learn to listen -

• it is necessary to learn how to hear from God - with practice
• we must learn to seek with all our heart Jer 29:11-13
• we must wait on him spending time in his Presence Is 40:31
• we need to read the Word regularly and develop the practice of fellowship and responding to the voice of the Holy Spirit Ps 89:15-17; Pro 8:33-35; Gal 5:25.

3:10-21 Speak, LORD, for your servant is listening – this is the attitude and response of those who wish to hear from God.

Many see prayer merely as a means of achieving what we want. God wants to mould, shape and direct us for the greater good and for his service - he is more interested in our character than in our comfort. We need to be prepared to act when he directs.

Eli recognized the sovereignty of God v18. God spoke through Samuel and the people recognized his anointing v19-21.

The Ark Captured by the Philistines

4:1-18 In the time before Samuel came to leadership Israel fought against the Philistines at Aphek and were defeated. The elders decided to bring the Ark as a mascot - they did not inquire of the LORD. Eli's two irreverent sons were involved. We must understand that physical symbols are of no help in our walk with the LORD. God is Spirit and blesses those who commit to him with all their heart and at all times, not just in the time of need.

The Ark was captured - 30,000 were killed, including Eli's sons v11. When Eli heard the news he died. He led Israel for forty years v18.

4:19-22 **The Glory Departed from Israel** As a result of the arrogance and disobedience of the people the Presence of the LORD was no longer with them. When the Ark was lost to the Philistines God abandoned Shiloh as the place where the LORD appeared to the people Jos 18:1; Ps 78:60. The Tabernacle and Altar of Burnt Offering were relocated to Nob north of Jerusalem possibly by Samuel 21:1 and were at Gibeon by the reign of David 1Chr 16:39; 21:29. The glory of God will depart if we do not honor him in our lives, homes, church and country.

5:1-12 **God's Presence in the Philistine Cities** The capture of the Ark was considered a great triumph by the idol worshiping Philistines so they placed it before their idol as a symbol of victory. Twice the idol fell before the Presence of the LORD. When he returns *every knee will bow and every tongue confess that Jesus Christ is LORD Phil 2:10,11.* The people were afflicted with plague v6. They decided to move it to other cities and in each case the people suffered with plague v9. The rulers returned the Ark to Israel – the LORD does not need anyone to defend him! v11. It is our privilege that the LORD allows us to work with him and includes us in what he is doing.

6:1-12 **The Ark returned to Israel** After only seven months the Philistines sent the Ark back to Israel in fear and trembling! Who can stand in the Presence of the LORD? They sought advice to make sure it was done in the right way. Beth Shemesh was 15 km west of Jerusalem on the way to Shiloh.

6:13-21 The Levites took down the Ark of the LORD It was placed on a rock and they made sacrifices of thanksgiving according to the Law. *They looked into the Ark* After the festivities people treated the Ark with disrespect and were struck down Num 4:5. In fear the Ark was moved 10 km along the road to Kiriath Jearim.

7:1,2 **The Ark remained** there for 80 years till recovered by David 2Sam 6:1,2. Abinadab consecrated Eleazer to guard it.

Samuel as Judge

7:3–12 **Samuel became judge** after the death of Eli around 1080 BC. When the people agreed to return to the LORD Samuel demanded they get rid of the foreign idols and genuinely commit to God. We may call on God when in need. But he calls us to genuine dedication every day of our lives. Samuel assembled Israel at Mizpah 4 km west of Jerusalem where they fasted and confessed their sin as Samuel interceded for them. When the Philistines knew they were gathered there, they attacked. Samuel called on the LORD. Even while he was praying God answered by causing panic so that the Philistines were routed. The prayer of faith is powerful Jas. 5:16-18.

7:13-17 **Peace in Israel** Samuel was established as judge for 30 years. The Philistines were subdued, land was restored and peace established under the hand of God.

Samuel traveled a regular circuit of 40 km from **Bethel** to **Gilgal** to **Mizpah** and returned to his home in **Ramah** where he built an altar. There was no attempt to restore Shiloh after it had been abandoned or to return the Ark there Ps 78:60; Jer 7:12. Samuel is credited with forming the school of prophets 2Kin 2:1-5; 4:38-41. He was held in high honor before God Jer 15:1.

END OF THEOCRACY - BEGINNING OF MONARCHY

Israel Requested a King The people of Israel were chosen by God. They were redeemed out of the world to be his treasured possession, a kingdom of priests and a holy nation for him. He was their King. He brought them on eagle's wings and called them into his Presence on Mt Sinai Ex 19:4-6. But their desire for independence turned awe into fear and they withdrew from God Ex 20:18-21. They never reached their potential - always withdrawing from God, choosing to be like the people of the world. This same attitude is prevalent today.

8:1-22 Now appoint a king to lead us As Samuel grew old his sons became judges but were dishonest, perverting justice. Since the time of Moses Israel was led by God through the judges.

They have rejected me v7. This was a further attempt to be free from the authority of God over their lives. The demand for a king did not come from God yet – *he gave them what they asked for, but sent leanness into their soul Ps 106:15.* We must be aware that our choices may lead us away from God. He wants a direct relationship with each of us as individuals, made possible now by the death of Jesus Heb 10:19. Samuel's faith is demonstrated as he continued to act on behalf of the people even when they had rejected God v22.

Samuel told them the burdens a king would place on them v11. Compare this with the blessings promised by God if they would commit their ways to him Deu 28:1-14. This choice remains with us today! We may commit our lives to Jesus and allow him to direct our path. Or we may choose to live by the ways of the world and our own independent judgment. God's promises are before us and open to all who seek Prov 3:5-12; Mt 6:31-34.

The people refused to listen – an action they would regret. God allowed the monarchy in order to prove the inability of man to lead his own destiny v22. This is still apparent in the conflict, corruption, persecution and injustice in the nations today.

SAUL CHOSEN AS KING 1050-1010 BC – 40 years

9:1,2 The Sovereignty of God Although the choice for a king was made by the people yet God was in control. He would demonstrate the frailty of human nature. The first king God selected met worldly standards. He was impressive, a popular choice! Within a short time he would fail 13:13,14.

God's standards are different to those of the world 16:7.

9:3-27 The incident concerning the donkeys showed Saul's lack of spiritual insight. God gave them what they asked for – what could they have become if they had been faithful!

10:1-16 Saul was anointed by Samuel. *The Spirit of the LORD will come upon you v6* – he was changed into a different person. All who are committed to God's service need the ongoing filling of the Holy Spirit to empower them for the task Acts 1:8. He will be given to the humble and obedient Acts 5:32.

God changed Saul's heart v9. God will change us to achieve the tasks he calls us to undertake if we are willing.

10:17-27 Samuel assembled the people and reminded them of the cost of having a king v17. He then appointed Saul the first king of Israel. He continued as priest. Saul went to his home in Gibeah 10 km north of Jerusalem.

11:1-15 **Saul's First Victory** The Ammonites attacked the town of Jabesh Gilead east of Jordan. Israel now had a king to appeal to for protection – at least they were united. *The Spirit of the LORD came on him in power v6.* Saul raised an army and defeated the Ammonites. As a result he was confirmed as king. This was the beginning of the **United Kingdom**.

Samuel's Farewell Message

12:1-25 With the appointment of Saul as king Samuel was no longer leader (judge). He would remain as priest before God.

• Samuel confronted the people about the faithfulness of God in bringing them to this point as a nation in the Promised Land
• he reminded them that it was their decision to have a king
• in so doing they were rejecting the direct rule of God v12
• it was evil because God was their King 10:19; 12:16-17
• despite their desire for independence they could still receive the blessing of God on their lives if they and their king would fear and serve the LORD
• thunder and rain came down to confirm his words v18.

Far be it from me that I should sin by failing to pray for you – we must never give up in praying for those the LORD lays on our hearts v23.

Saul's Independence

13:1 **Beginning of the Downfall** Saul could have been a good king. He had the worldly attributes, was modest and unassuming with the anointing of God. He responded to the Holy Spirit and acted decisively in his first challenge 11:6. However he did not inquire of God before taking action. He did not honor God or God's Word. He became proud, independent and disobedient to God's commands Deu 17:18-20. We must always remember that success is due to our dependence on God and not on our own efforts. When we become unresponsive to God's leading the Spirit withdraws 1Thes 5:19.

***13:2-13* Conflict continued with the Philistines** Saul set up two army posts at Micmash and Bethel. This was some 20 years into his reign as Jonathan his son was now a military leader. Nothing is recorded of this intervening period.

Jonathan led an attack on a Philistine outpost stirring the enemy and causing the army to be marshaled v3.

The troops were afraid as they waited for Samuel to come and bless them. Often we are asked to wait on God as a test of faith 10:8. Samuel was still priest and responsible for representing the people before God. When he was delayed Saul presumptuously took action into his own hands and offered the sacrifice himself, contrary to God's command. He did not inquire of the LORD and failed the test. Samuel passed judgment on Saul v11.

I thought - I felt compelled to offer the burnt offering v12 We should not be led entirely by our thoughts or by the urgency of the situation, but by the Word of God and our faith. If Saul had obeyed God he could have retained the kingdom. Because of his independence it was lost to him and his family v13.

***13:13,14* God's Standard** Saul was selected by worldly standards 9:1. Now David was chosen by God's standard 16:7.

The LORD has sought out a man after his own heart v14 – he was a ten year old boy! *The eyes of the LORD range throughout the earth to strengthen those whose hearts are fully committed to him 2Chr 16:9.* May we be fully committed in our hearts.

13:15-22 There was no decisive victory - Israel continued to be subject to the Philistines throughout Saul's reign v16.

Jonathan's Leadership

14:1-46 One of the sad consequences of Saul's disobedience was that his courageous son, who had so much potential suffered. Jonathan once again took the initiative, a step of faith –

Courage, Zeal and Faith – *Come let's go - Nothing can hinder the LORD from saving, whether by many or by few v6.* Some people have a desire to achieve. They are motivated by the hunt! While nine may explain why it can't be done there is one who will be doing it. They see a problem as an opportunity, a challenge as a step in the plan. Motivation is a major factor in achievement - good motivation produces commitment, contribution and success - poor motivation results in compliance, conformity, discouragement and failure. Jonathan was self-motivated, he had courage and zeal - he was an achiever. He also had faith in God. A sign of faith is confidence in God's ability to act and deliver. Faith becomes real when it results in action that requires God's assistance.

As a result of Jonathan's step of faith panic broke out in the Philistine camp – a panic sent by God v15. Saul was more interested in finding the cause of victory than in participating – he took a roll call and discovered it was his son's bravery. 'Ark' should read 'ephod', by which the priest sought guidance v18. Saul made a foolish vow v24 - it brought hunger on the soldiers and caused them to eat unprepared meat v33. He built an altar without Samuel's presence and sought instruction from God but received no reply. By casting lots he found that Jonathan was victim of a second foolish vow v39. The soldiers would not allow Jonathan to be harmed v45.

14:47-52 Israel was chosen by God but in rebelling against him they had continued conflict despite Saul's efforts.

Rejection of Saul as King

15:1-35 **To obey is better than sacrifice** v22 Saul was given one last chance to obey God. He was told to totally destroy the Amalekites for their affliction of Israel when they first tried to enter the Promised Land Num 14:45. He was successful in defeating them but spared their king and the best of the livestock. This was the final act of arrogant defiance against God. Despite Saul's justification Samuel said *to obey is better than sacrifice v22.* Saul begged to be forgiven. He was told *He who is the Glory of Israel does not lie or change his mind v29.* This was the end of Samuel's support for Saul v34,35.

DAVID ANOINTED AS FUTURE KING

16:1-23 God chose David to contrast against the failure of Saul. *The LORD does not look at the things man looks at. Man looks at the outward appearance, but the LORD looks at the heart v7.* This is encouragement to those who would serve God. The attitude of our heart towards God is what counts rather than the opinions of mankind. David was chosen by God as *a man after his own heart 13:14.* He was ten years old at the time!

The Spirit of the LORD came upon David in power v13. We can expect God's anointing power for service through the filling of the Holy Spirit Acts 2:4. David was responsive to the anointing. Anointing with oil signifies the covering by God.

Saul was tormented by an evil spirit. David as a youth was brought to entertain him v18. By this time David was already recognized for his courage. He pleased Saul and remained in his service for some time.

David's Faith

17:1-58 **The Fall of Goliath** The Philistines mounted a major war against Israel and set camp at Socoh, thirty km west of Jerusalem. A champion named Goliath challenged Israel to choose a representative but all were terrified. David had returned to his father's care while his older brothers were enlisted. He visited them at camp and heard the challenge of Goliath v23.

Who is this - that he should defy the armies of the living God? v26. Saul and his men saw the physical situation – a giant.

David saw one who defied God. We must learn to see things from the spiritual side and be confident that God will always defend his name.

•   David's confidence and declaration of faith were based on his relationship and past experience with God v34-36 - small beginnings prepare us for greater things

•   He would not be intimidated by the doubts and fears, opinions or negative attitudes of others v28,29,33

•   He would not use another's weapons, only what he had v40.

•   He knew God could do what he had done in the past v37.

We need not live under the circumstances. Every situation is sent to test our faith and prepare us for future tasks the LORD has in store for us. We can rise above circumstances when we are guided by God's past acts and his Word. Faith and victory came from David's personal walk with the LORD - his experience with sheep taught him to depend on the Shepherd Ps 23.

I come against you in the name of the LORD Almighty – whom you have defied v45 We must always stand in God's name for the battle is the LORD's. There is boldness for those who know his Presence. That David chose five stones when only one was needed demonstrates the practical side of faith - we make our plan and then commit our trust to God.

David seized the opportunity to act quickly and decisively – he ran to the Philistine, he felled him then decapitated him. Israel had a resounding victory. Saul had forgotten the former service of David v55. David kept the weapons of Goliath as was his right. The head he took to Jerusalem v54. Did he have the future conquest of Jerusalem in mind?

Saul's Jealousy of David

18:1-30 Jonathan's friendship as the king's son grew to protect David from his father's wrath. Saul again kept David at his residence. ***Whatever Saul sent him to do, David did it so successfully v5.*** David's success made Saul jealous to the point of attempting to kill him v10. Good leaders learn to use capable people to the full extent of their ability rather than throw spears.

In everything he did he had great success because the LORD was with him v14. The reason for his success was his faith and commitment to God. Ps 71:5,14-17. We can know success as we walk with God. His Presence is all we need - it is available as we seek him daily Ps 89:15-17. Saul used his daughter to cause David's death in battle v20,21. Their love for each other only deepened Saul's jealousy as David's popularity grew.

19:1-24 Saul's jealousy became an obsession to kill David. Jonathan and Michal both acted to protect David until he was forced to flee to Samuel at Ramah v18. Despite Saul's efforts God kept David safe v23.

20:1-42 David sought further help from Jonathan v1.

Enmity restricts a leader's ability to utilize valuable resources. David could have been Saul's most valuable asset. Instead he became a distraction from duty. The task of a leader is to identify and use ability in the best interests of the person and organization by assisting the person to rise to their maximum level of competency. Saul's jealousy and self-centeredness made him blind to the resource at his disposal. David realized he must leave Saul's presence rather than throw spears in return v42.

David's Flight from Saul

21:1-15 **In Nob and Gath** David went alone to the local town of Nob where the priests had set up the Tabernacle after the Ark had been taken from Shiloh. He asked Ahimelech the priest to seek God's guidance for him and also took the showbread and the sword of Goliath. David then went to Gath, a Philistine city 40 km southwest of Jerusalem to seek refuge but was recognized and rejected. His trust in God at this time is recorded Ps 68.

THE MAKING OF A KING

22:1-5 **The Cave of Adullam** David set up a base in a cave at Adullam, some 20 km from Jerusalem. Why was it necessary for David to undergo such a rigorous apprenticeship? God requires that character and leadership ability be refined in the crucible of life's experiences 1Pet 1:6,7 -

- vision is shaped and confirmed through application
- authority must be experienced to be exercised
- diligence must be shown in all activities - as to the LORD
- integrity must be demonstrated before God and man
- persistence and learning are developed through all situations – both good and bad – your own and that of others
- Recognition of the sovereignty of God in all circumstances develops 2Sam 15:25,26
- a leader must learn to serve, before and after appointment Mt 20:25-28.

All God's Great Leaders learned leadership through adversity and hardship - Moses in Midian Ex 3:1; Joseph in prison Gen 37-47 - Jesus *learned obedience from what he suffered and once made perfect Heb 5:8-10.* David became a great king because he learned to serve God under Saul.

Building a Team v2 Many people who were dissatisfied with Saul including David's family came to him. Despite their rebellious nature they gradually followed David because of who he was. He forged them into a fighting force of 400.

Leaders must learn to get the best out of people – to help each person reach their maximum potential. Remember that your success may depend on their contribution. We learn from poor examples as well as good.

He went to Moab to obtain security for his parents (his great-grandmother Ruth was from Moab) v3.

THE FAILURE OF A LEADER

22:6-23 **Self-centered Obsession** In a senseless act Saul's inadequacies, fear and madness caused him to kill the 85 priests of Nob and their families for assisting David. Only one priest, Abiathar escaped with the ephod and he went to join David. The **ephod** was a special vest used by the priest in worship and prayer for guidance Ex 28:6,29,30; Lev 8:7,8.

At this, perhaps the lowest point in his flight from Saul David wrote - *my heart is steadfast, O God Ps 57:7.* The magnitude of his circumstances from which he rose is recorded in Ps 142:1-7.

23:1-29 **Inquiring of the LORD** David defended the nearby town of Keilah, a role Saul should have undertaken. He frequently inquired of the LORD – this was a major factor in his success. He also used the ephod. He applied the spiritual disciplines of growth Acts 2:42-47. Saul continued his insane pursuit of David v7. With God's guidance David remained free - he kept moving from place to place with a number of strongholds.

He found strength in God v16 Strong spiritual friends are important as we find our strength in God Pro 27:17. David finally resided in the stronghold of En Gedi on the shore of the Dead Sea v29. Leadership is forged in the school of brokenness - until one is nothing, God can do nothing with them.

I sing in the shadow of your wings One of the most beautiful expressions of the personal walk with God was written in the desert of Judea - it is a life-guide for all who would walk with the LORD Ps 63:1-11.

Integrity Before God

24:1-22 The LORD forbid that I should - lift my hand against - the anointed of the Lord v6 David was given opportunity to take Saul's life in a cave – he refused to do it. We must respect those whom God has placed in authority. We may not always agree but we must accept authority Ps 105:15. It also demonstrates that David learned to handle hardship without bitterness or resentment as he submitted to God's discipline.

25:1 **Death of Samuel** - around 1025 BC

25:2-44 David moved to the desert of Maon, forty km south of Jerusalem. He moved frequently not only for safety but to find food for his people. This he obtained by protecting the towns of Israel or by attacking their enemies. He asked for provisions from a wealthy local and was refused. He determined to take what he needed but was prevented by the intervention of the man's wife who diverted David from vengeance v28. She had a prophetic word for David v29. After the death of her husband Abigail became David's wife.

26:1-25 The LORD rewards every man for his righteousness and faithfulness v23 David again spared Saul's life – he was submitted to the sovereignty of God. This truth is based on God's character and is true today though faith and perseverance may be required to see its fulfilment, as in the case of David who continually submitted to God. In all the circumstances of life we must understand that God is developing our character v9-11.

27:1-12 Despite the words of Saul, David realized he must move from Saul's reach so he sought refuge again in the Philistine city of Gath v1.

He was given access to the town of Ziklag, a further thirty km south. He continued to attack the enemies of Israel for food.

The Downfall of Saul

28:1-25 A problem arose when the Philistines next attacked Israel and David was expected to fight with them. When Saul saw the Philistine army he was afraid and inquired of the LORD but no answer was given v6. He then consulted a medium to bring Samuel back from the dead. This showed how far Saul had fallen from fellowship with God. The experience was a bad one - he was told he and his sons would die the next day!

David's Continued Faith

29:1-11 David was saved from fighting against Israel because of the distrust of the Philistine commanders. Sometimes we have to move ahead in uncertainty and trust that God will open a way of escape Rom 8:28; 1Cor 10:13.

30:1-31 **Disaster turned to Victory** Instead of having to join the battle against Israel David returned to Ziklag - to find his town sacked. ***David found strength in the LORD his God v6.*** No matter how bad a situation is we can find strength in God - *my God will meet all your needs according to his glorious riches in Christ Jesus Phil 4:19;* Is 40:31. As always, David inquired of God and was told to pursue the Amalekite raiders v8. He gathered his disgruntled resources and led them to victory v6,9. They rescued the families, recovered their possessions and took the plunder of the enemy. David ruled that all should share alike v24. He even sent gifts to the elders of Judah (his family tribe).

The Death of Saul

31:1-13 Israel fought against the Philistines at Mt Gilboa seventy km north of Jerusalem and were defeated. Saul took his own life. His body was fastened to the wall of nearby Beth Shan. The sad end of this king with so much potential was worsened by the deaths of his courageous sons.

2 Samuel – 'asked of God'

Introduction – After the deaths of Samuel and Saul the record continues with the reign of David and the securing of the United Kingdom of Israel. So much detail is given to the life of David because of his importance in displaying character and qualities that are commendable to God 1Sam 13:14; 16:7. We can learn much from the faithfulness of David, a man after God's heart, who was a great king and also the forerunner of Jesus the King of kings Rev 19:16.

While David was a good king his failures are also recorded.

Author – It was the practice of leaders in most cultures to record significant deeds 8:16.

Period – David came to the throne of Judah, his own tribe around 1010 BC after the death of Saul. He was made king over all Israel in 1003 and ruled till 970 BC.

Theme – The monarchy was consolidated with the reign of David He demonstrated faith in his commitment to God.

Promise of the Messiah Following David's faithfulness God promised that his throne would be established forever by the Messiah foretold by the prophets 7:12-16; Is 9:7 - to be fulfilled by the Second Coming of Jesus.

SUMMARY
David Established as King 1:1 to 5:5
David's First Acts as King 5:6 to 6:23
A House for the LORD 7:1-29
David's Victories 8:1 to 10:19
David's Failure and Repentance 11:1 to 12:31
Consequence of Sin 13:1 to 19:43
Final Years 20:1 to 24:25
Reason for the Monarchy

DAVID ESTABLISHED AS KING
King over Judah 1010-970 BC – 40 years
1:1-27 **A time of mourning** David genuinely mourned the death of Saul and Jonathan showing his respect for Saul and his love for Jonathan.

He also gave thanks to God for protection during his flight from Saul - *You, O LORD, keep my lamp burning! Ps 18:28.*

2:1 David inquired of God about his next move. We often turn to God in times of trouble and need. Our relationship must extend to the good times as well - this was a reason for David's success – he prayed over the big issues of life Ps 37:4-7.

2:2-7 King in Hebron In prayer he was told to go to Hebron the major town of Judah, thirty km south of Jerusalem. He was made king over his own tribe of Judah and Joab led the army.

2:8-32 No capable king in Israel There was no competent surviving heir from Saul's family. Abner, commander of the army of Israel made Ish-Bosheth, Saul's son king over the northern tribes. Conflict remained between north and south for seven years. Abner was forced to kill Joab's brother Asahel in battle for which Joab swore revenge v23. What did the conflict achieve for the people? We must speak out against division in the church v26. We must make every effort to keep the unity the Spirit brings Eph 4:3.

3:1-5 David increased in strength as the northern coalition weakened. He had six sons of his six wives.

3:6-21 Peace with Israel The leaders of Israel came to recognize that the anointing of the LORD was on David v17. So Abner then decided to give his allegiance to David and reached an agreement with him v21.

3:22-39 Further conflict Joab was not involved in the agreement and took revenge by killing Abner v27; 2:20-23. David showed remorse at the death of Abner which pleased the people and demonstrated the genuine nature of David's dealings. Joab was later killed by Solomon for this act 1Kin 2:5,6,34.

4:1-12 With the death of Abner, Ish-Bosheth lost support and was murdered by his two sons.

DAVID - KING OVER ALL ISRAEL 1003-970 BC - 33 years

5:1-5 Israel came to David at Hebron He became king of Judah at thirty years of age where he reigned seven years. He was made king over all Israel for a further thirty-three years. He was anointed king as a youth possibly around 10 years old 1Sam 16:13. This means that despite his early fame and success he had to wait some twenty years to achieve the promise. During that time he was moulded to be the man who would be a great king. We must be patient as we wait for God's time knowing there is a purpose in every event.

DAVID'S FIRST ACTS AS KING

5:6-16 Jerusalem Conquered David's first act was to take the Jebusite city of Jerusalem and establish it as Zion, capital of Israel. This unconquered city of Benjamin was neutral on the border between Judah and the other northern states of Israel. It is of great significance in the history of Israel and the world -

- The city of Melchizedek king of Salem (peace) Gen 14:18
- It is Mt Moriah, where God tested Abraham Gen 22:2
- Abraham prophesied calling it YHWH Jireh 'on the mountain of the LORD it will be provided' Gen 22:8,14. This prophecy was fulfilled there at Calvary when the Lamb of God was crucified for our sin Jn 19:17
- It was not conquered since the time of Moses Jos 10:1; 15:63
- Zion was the Jebusite name for 'citadel – safe place'. It became Zion, the City of David v7. The foundations of the supporting terraces are still evident today. It was to be known as Zion, dwelling place of God Ps 76:1,2
- It was where God halted the plague and the site of the Temple that Solomon, son of David would build 2Chr 3:1
- It was to this place that David took the head of Goliath to commemorate his first great victory! 1Sam 17:54
- The water shaft built by Hezekiah and used by David to gain access to Jerusalem was discovered in 1867 v6-8; 2Kin 20:20
- It will be the name of the new eternal Jerusalem Rev 21:2.

David knew that his success was for the sake of God's people. We must always recognize this fact in our service v12; Mt 20:25-28; Jn 13:12-17. *God opposes the proud but gives grace to the humble Jas 4:6.*
David's children included Solomon and Nathan – both included in the royal line of Jesus v13-16; 3:2-5; Mt 1:6; Lk 3:31.

5:17-25 Nations subdued The Philistines attacked David and he did as the LORD commanded him – he struck them down and subdued them v19, 23, 25. Because of his faithfulness, trust and commitment he was able to achieve what Saul and the Judges could not do.

The Ark of the LORD brought to Jerusalem

6:1-11 Having gained peace in Israel David sought to honor God by bringing the Ark to Jerusalem from the house of Abinadab where it had been for eighty years. The Ark was lost in battle and was returned after causing trouble for the Philistines but only as far as Kiriath Jearim 1Sam 4:11; 6:21. David's intention was to unite the political and religious life of Israel by putting God and the Ark at the center of the nation. This showed his devotion to God as the Ark represented God's Presence.

In their enthusiasm they forgot the procedures required to respect the things of God v7. The method of moving the Ark on a cart was contrary to God's instructions Ex 25:14. Uzzah showed contempt for the holiness of God and died because of his irreverent act Num 4:15, 20. While celebrating the freedom of salvation we must also *worship God acceptably with reverence and awe for our 'God is a consuming fire' Heb 12:28,29.*

How can the Ark of the LORD come to me v9 David was both angry and afraid. He learned a new reverence for God. He left the Ark with Obed-Edom for three months. When the household was blessed David then decided to bring the Ark to Jerusalem, this time using the right procedure 1Chr 15:13.

6:12-23 They brought the Ark of the LORD and set it in its place inside the tent David had pitched v17 David had prepared a Tabernacle for the Ark in Jerusalem north of his residence (the old one at Shiloh was disgraced). He took the role of priest and offered sacrifices of thanksgiving to God – this shows God's acceptance of David and the closeness of David's walk and his relationship with God. This is now available to all through Jesus.

When he returned home his wife was critical of his behavior but David maintained that his joy was in the LORD v21.

A HOUSE FOR THE LORD

7:1-17 David wanted to build a house (building) for the Ark. This was not an idea that came from God! The Ark and the Tabernacle only represented the Presence of God. It is God's intention to dwell in the heart of the believer. Nathan the prophet told David that *the Lord himself will establish a house v11.*

The House God Has Planned will be an eternal kingdom of people of all nations. It will be set up by one of David's offspring. Ultimately that One is the Lord Jesus Christ –

• *He is the one who will build a house for my Name and I will establish the throne of his kingdom forever v13-16*
• *The LORD God will give him the throne of his father David – his kingdom will never end Lk 1:32, 33*
• *He will reign on David's throne forever Is 9:7*
• From this man's descendants God has brought to Israel the Savior Jesus as he promised Acts 13:22,23
• The believer who receives Jesus as Savior and LORD is a member of that spiritual household 1Chr 17:1-15; 1Pet 2:5
• There will be no *temple in the city, because the LORD God Almighty and the Lamb are its temple Rev 21:22.*

7:18-29 A Prayer of Thanksgiving for God's promise of an eternal kingdom of all nations. David showed his devotion and reverence towards the Sovereign LORD in this prayer of humility, praise and trust.

DAVID'S VICTORIES

8:1-18 The LORD gave David victory wherever he went David gained control over all the Promised Land as had been promised to Abraham 900 years before Gen 15:18-21 -

• Philistines – on the south west coast, enemies since the days of the conquest v1; 5:17-25; Jud 3:2-3
• Moab – east of the Dead Sea, descendants of Lot and antagonistic to Israel v2
• Aram (Damascus, Syria) – north of Israel v3-8; 10:15-19
• Edom – south of the Dead Sea, descendants of Esau v14
• Ammon – east of the Jordan River 10:6-19; 12:26-31
• from the southern desert to the Euphrates v3.

David led Israel to achieve fulfilment of the promise by removing all idols and taking them from a chaotic group of tribes to an integrated nation with a dynasty of kings that would last in Judah for 424 years – it will continue into eternity.

His commitment to God also allowed the establishment of an eternal dynasty, fulfilled in the coming of Jesus Christ.

In the midst of the battle David wrote *with God we will gain the victory and he will trample down our enemies Ps 60:12* - we can know this confidence as well.

9:1-13 An Act of Kindness David showed his character by including Mephibosheth, a son of Jonathan at the king's table.

10:1-19 Conflict with Ammon David extended friendship to the nations around Israel. The new king of Ammon abused David's delegates resulting in war. Joab lead Israel in this battle while David remained in Jerusalem.

DAVID'S FAILURE AND REPENTANCE

11:1-27 David displeased the LORD For all David's greatness the Bible records that he was subject to significant failures. While he was active in conquest and building the nation of Israel he prospered. As he aged around 50 years old, he withdrew from the conflict and service. Had he continued to be active for God this series of events may not have occurred. Busy minds focus on the task – idle hands court temptation Gen 4:6,7; 1Cor 10:11,12.

David was drawn to desire Bathsheba, the wife of Uriah, one of his commanders. She became pregnant and David devised a plan to have Uriah killed. When we feed the desires of the eyes and heart they materialize and multiply. We must *set our hearts and minds on the things above where Christ is seated at the right hand of God Col 3:1.*

David's acts of adultery and murder went unpunished for twelve months. His position and authority prevented a challenged.

12:1-12 Sin Exposed Nathan, the prophet brought a hypothetical case to David for judgment. David ruled against the offender only to be told it was himself – *you are the man! v7.*

I would have given you more v9 God had made David a successful and great king, granted him all the desires of his heart and would have given him more.

Broken Fellowship How did David live for the period before the disclosure of his sin? He must have withdrawn from regular fellowship with God during that time. This is a warning - we need our time with the LORD each day to keep us on track - God's Word will keep us from sin or sin will keep us from God's Word 2Tim 3:16. Remember to apply the spiritual disciplines of prayer, reading the Word, worship, fellowship and witnessing - they maintain a strong walk; their neglect leads to distraction Ps 1:1-6; Acts 2:42-47; 1Pet 5:8.

Why did you despise the Word of the LORD by doing what is evil in his eyes? v9. We are accountable to God as individuals. He requires that we walk with him daily and obey his Word. One day we will be required to answer this question.

12:13–17 **Repentance** – *I have sinned against the LORD v13* Despite the gravity of his sin against Uriah and Bathsheba and the nation David recognized his sin was primarily against God.

The extent of David's repentance is portrayed in Psalm 51 -
- a plea for mercy without rights v1
- recognition of the offense of sin to God v3-6
- confession – to come into agreement with God v4
- a desire to be cleansed, forgiven, restored v7
- repentance – a commitment to turn from sin v10
- an attitude of humility - a broken spirit and a contrite heart v17; Mt 5:3.

David's great fear was that he would be cast from the Presence of God and the Holy Spirit and that he would lose the joy of salvation v11,12. His awareness of the Spirit of God conforms with the daily encounter of the born again believer Gal 5:22.

12:18-25 **Forgiveness** Only God can forgive, remove the stain of sin and restore to a renewed relationship. Once the time of genuine repentance was over David could return to fellowship with God v20. This is the extent of **God's grace and mercy!** We can come back from failure. Although the first son died a second son was born - Solomon who became the next king.

12:26-31 **Ammon Subdued** The battle which David failed to join and where Uriah was murdered drew to a conclusion. At the point of victory Joab called David to attend to conquer the Ammonite city of Rabbah.

The Consequences of Sin
There were seven significant consequences of David's sin -

12:18 The son born to Bathsheba died - *consequence 1.*

13:1-22 David's daughter Tamar was unnecessarily defiled and shamefully abused by his firstborn son Ammon - *consequence 2.*

13:23-39 Absalom, David's third son murdered his brother in revenge for the mistreatment of his sister - *consequence 3.*

14:1-33 Absalom fled from Jerusalem and lived in exile.

15:1-12 He raised a revolt against David - *consequence 4.*
He stole the hearts of Israel by flattery and convinced many of them to make him king in Hebron v10.

***15:13-23* In humility David chose to leave Jerusalem** rather than fight his own son – with his family and all his officials he moved across the Jordan to Mahanaim on the Jabbok River 15:14. At this time he wrote *but you are a shield around me,O LORD; you bestow glory on me and lift up my head Ps 3:3.*

15:24-37* *If I find favor in the LORD's eyes he will bring me back David held the anointing lightly. If we can't trust God with our anointing it is not genuine. David did not know God's will at this time and was prepared to allow God's sovereignty to be revealed. When uncertain, trust God!

16:1-14 During his flight David was met by the servant of Mephibosheth who falsely gained David's favor v3. One of Saul's relatives also met David and cursed him v5.

16:15-23 Absalom brought shame on David by defiling his concubines - *consequence 5.*

17:1-29 Absalom accepted bad advice and gathered a large army before pursuing David giving him time to regroup and prepare his army to defend 17:8.

18:1-5 David assembled his own men for battle against Absalom but they would not let him join them to protect his life v1. The king asked that his son be spared v5.

18:6-18 Absalom was killed by Joab in the nearby forest even though David's army was victorious - *consequence 6.*

18:19-33 David mourned greatly over the death of Absalom.

19:1-8 Despite the victory over Absalom David had to be chastened by Joab – ***now go out and encourage your men*** v7. This is a fundamental principle of leadership - to recognize, encourage and motivate each person. A leader must not allow personal feelings to influence his actions or behavior. While feelings and emotion can be used to achieve results they must not be allowed to distort judgment or response.
David's sorrow was in part due to his own failures.

19:9-43 David returned to Jerusalem and after some destabilizing influence peace and unity was regained. David was restored as king and wisely showed mercy to those who had wronged him v22.

19:13 The event concerning the death of Absalom turned David against Joab his military commander - *consequence 7.* Because he murdered Absalom Joab was replaced as commander of the army by Amasa who was later murdered by Joab 20:10. The senseless enmity between David and Joab resulted in Joab's execution under Solomon 1Kin 2:5,6,34.

THE FINAL YEARS

20:1-26 **Further Rebellion and Conflict** Another leader took the opportunity to rise against David but his army soon put down the rebellion.

Note the recorder and secretary of the king's business v24,25.

21:1-22 **Break with the Past** There was a three year famine and David sought the LORD. It was due to Saul's massacre of the Gibeonites (not recorded) - they were under protection Jos 9:26,27. David rectified the matter. When Saul's body had been properly put to rest *God answered prayer in behalf of the land* – the consequence of Saul's broken relationship with God was borne by the people v14. There were a number of wars with the Philistines and David was protected by his mighty men v15-22.

22:1-51 **David's Song of Praise** David's confidence in God is evident. He will be remembered before God not for his achievements and failures but for his faith and trust in God Heb 11:32. This is an example for us - we can have the same faith and trust – we can take this song as our own -
• God was his rock, deliverer, refuge, shield, stronghold v2,3; Ex 33:21-23
• in the midst of all his deep troubles God saved him v4-7
• he gloried in the majesty of God, in creation and his life v8-20
• he found God's ways to be perfect and God's Word to be flawless v31,32
• he recognized his skills and success came from God v33-37
• he had a relationship with God - his Rock and Savior! v47-51.

23:1-7 **Confidence in Death** David's last words – he acknowledged he was exalted and anointed by the Most High and Israel's beloved singer - he is credited with 73 of the 150 Psalms. He looked forward to eternal life v5,

23:8-39 **David's Mighty Men** As a great leader David attracted and trained mighty men, three in particular and two others v17,18,20. There were also thirty, including Uriah, the husband of Bathsheba 1Chr 11:41.

Leaders must get the best out of their people - help each to achieve their full potential.

***24:1-17* The Plague of Pride** A census was taken which brought a plague. It was due to pride and self-dependence - relying on numbers rather than the LORD v3. He was given three options and chose to fall into the hands of God v12. The plague was stopped. Leaders must take responsibility for issues – the people are but sheep! v17.

***24:18-25* Site of the Temple** 1Chr 22:1-19 The LORD told David to build an altar on the threshing floor of Araunah, the Jebusite where the plague stopped some km from his residence v18. David bought the land, built an altar and made an offering to God. Do not offer to the LORD what costs us nothing v24.

Mt Moriah This site is the historic Mt Moriah where Abraham was called to offer his son, Isaac in an act of faith Gen 22:1-14. It was also the location where Solomon would build the Temple 2Sam 5:6-16; 2Chr 3:1. The Dome of the Rock now stands there.

This site is at the centre of Jerusalem and will be the scene of world significance in the end time Zec 8:1-3; Rev 11:1; 14:1.

Reason for the Monarchy
The request for a king did not come from God – each of the aspirations of the hearts of mankind must be tested to confirm the righteousness of God's ways. God allowed the monarchy to prove the failure of man to lead his own destiny 1Sam 8:22; 12:19; Pro 20:24; Jer 10:23. The people desired a king because of their unwillingness to submit to God and their inability to work together for the common good. Human nature is basically rebellious and needs to be subdued. Desire for freedom from constraint leads to independence from God. For people to live in unity requires humility, commitment, submission to God and acceptance of authority Eph 4:1-6; Phil 2:1-5.

The Books of Samuel show the principles and spiritual values on which a kingdom or nation must be established.

The Books of Kings show that power and unbridled authority lead to corruption, self-indulgence, pride, arrogance and rebellion against God Hos 8:4.

1 Kings

Introduction – The two Books of Kings were originally one. The United Kingdom of Israel established with the appointment of Saul 1Sam 11:1-15 rose to a position of power and expansion under David and Solomon subduing the neighboring nations with an empire reaching from the border of Egypt to the Euphrates River Jos 1:4; 1Kin 10:23; 2Chr 9:22-26. They then entered a time of political unrest and upheaval as great nations sought to control the Middle East – including Egypt, Assyria, Babylon and Persia. At the same time the people of Israel turned from God.

Kings begins with the Temple building and ends with its burning; begins with the Kingdom United and ends with no kingdom – the people in exile. The people failed because of the inability of human nature to abide by the Ten Commandments as a consequence of the fall of Adam.

Author – It was the practice of kings to record their significant acts for posterity with particular emphasis on their achievements such as the annals of Solomon 1Kin 11:41; annals of the kings of Judah 14:19 and annals of the kings of Israel 2Kin 14:28; 2Chr 16:11. These were the **official secular records.** The seers, scribes and kings recorders compiled these records many of which were lost 2Sam 8:16; 1Chr 29:29.

The Books of Kings however, were **specially written by the prophets** selecting specific events extracted from the official records to highlight God's dealings with the kings and people for good and bad to encourage future generations to honor God and live by his commandments. This would have been done in the time of the kings when the official records were still available.

Period – From the beginning of Solomon's reign 970 BC to the captivity 586 BC; a period of 384 years.

Theme – **The dividing of the Kingdom** The Books of Kings show how the Monarchy developed on human values with unfaithful kings. They record the demise of Israel from the pinnacle of prosperity and power under the early years of Solomon to the dispersion of Israel by Assyria and the exile of Judah by Babylon due to the failure of the kings and people to honor God and follow his ways. The captivity was predicted by Moses Deu 28:45-52.

1Kings The first 11 chapters record the reign of Solomon (40 years). His greatest achievement was the building of the Temple which confirmed the center of the Jewish faith in Jerusalem. Solomon was known for his legendary wisdom, immense wealth and enormous influence. He became king at 19 years of age and spent the first 20 years of his reign building the Temple and his palace as well as many other great building projects. However in the last ten years Solomon turned away from the LORD led astray by his many foreign wives. He incurred the anger of the LORD and the ten northern tribes were lost within a week of his death 11:1-13. He died a foolish king at the age of 59 - he accumulated horses from Egypt, took foreign wives and worshiped other gods 10:28; 11:1-13; 2Chr 9:28; Deu 17:16-20. **The rest of 1Kings** records the history of the Divided Kingdom (77 years) up to the appearance of God's miracle-working prophets Elijah and Elisha.

2Kings Covers the demise of Israel and Judah to the exile (267 years). The period of the monarchy confirmed the desire and need for a perfect king – a Messiah which was fulfilled in the coming of Jesus Lk 1:31-33.

SOLOMON SECURED AS KING 970-930 BC – 40 years

1:1-27 **A Leadership Challenge** When David reached 70 years of age his fourth son Adonijah sought to take the throne v5. He collaborated with Joab and Abiathar, two of David's key supporters. Quick action by Nathan the prophet avoided rebellion.

1:28-53 **David appointed Solomon** to become king. Born to Bathsheba he was possibly David's tenth son. Solomon was God's choice 1Chr 22:9 (to demonstrate that the greatest and most gifted among men can fall).

2:1-4 **David charged Solomon –** *show yourself a man and observe what the LORD requires v2,3.* Success would have continued under Solomon if he had followed this instruction.

2:5-46 David gave Solomon some scores to settle! Adonijah and Joab were executed. Benaiah became army commander and Zadok became priest v35.

Wisdom to Rule – a wise choice 2Chr 1:1-12

3:1-4 Solomon began an extensive building program - he *showed his love for the LORD by walking according to the statutes of his father David, except he offered sacrifices on the high places* rather than at the Ark v3. He chose popular extravagant celebrations over personal devotion 1Kin 11:7,8.

3:5-15 **The LORD appeared to Solomon** and gave him a request. He chose a discerning heart to govern the people v9. This pleased God who granted his request and promised him riches and honor as well v12-15.

3:16-28 Solomon's wisdom was confirmed in a wise judgment.

4:1-28 Solomon's Court The early period of Solomon's reign was the pinnacle of Israel's development and prosperity as a nation. He set up court administrators v1-6 and twelve district governors throughout the land v7-19. *Solomon ruled over all the kingdoms from the River Euphrates - as far as the border of Egypt. These countries brought tribute and were Solomon's subjects all his life.* The people *lived in safety, each man under his own vine and fig tree v21,25.*

4:29-34 Solomon's wisdom became legendary - he wrote 3,000 proverbs, 1,005 songs including the Song of Songs. He taught on many biological subjects and was widely consulted for his understanding.

BUILDING THE TEMPLE OF GOD

5:1-18 Preparations for building the Temple. The king of Tyre arranged to supply Solomon with the timber and craftsmen required.

6:1-38 The Temple was 27 m long x 9 m wide x 13.5 m high – designed to the proportions of the Tabernacle but twice the size v2 (14m x 4.5m x 5 m). It was begun in the fourth year of Solomon's reign - 966 BC and took seven years to build, dedicated in 959 BC v38.

7:1-12 Solomon's Palace was 46 m long x 23 m wide x 13.5 m high and took thirteen years to build. There was a throne room - the 'Hall of Justice' and a palace for Pharaoh's daughter v7,8.

7:13-51 Temple Furnishings - some dedicated by David v51.

8:1-9 *They brought up the Ark of the LORD and the Tent of Meeting* – these had been located by David close to his dwelling 2Sam 6:17. The Ark contained the two stone tablets given to Moses at Mt Sinai which represented the conditions of the Covenant God made with Israel v9.

8:10,11 The Glory of the LORD God revealed his splendor so intense that the priests could not perform their service.

8:12-66 Prayer of Dedication Solomon recalled the reason for building the Temple v14-21. He then dedicated the Temple defining the conditions for blessing and forgiveness v23-61.

9:1-9 The LORD Appeared After the Dedication when Solomon had achieved all he desired to do God answered v2. He had heard Solomon and put his Name in Jerusalem forever – **if Solomon remained faithful his throne would be secure**. But if he or his sons turned away from God the people would be exiled. Within thirty years Solomon would depart from this requirement. Despite the failure of people God's plan to dwell with mankind will be fulfilled, now through the Lord Jesus Christ.

Solomon's Fame

9:10-25 **Solomon's Business Activities** David left a secure kingdom with the surrounding nations subdued and a number paying tribute. For 20 years Solomon continued to build the prosperity of Israel with conscripted foreign labor. He also fulfilled the Temple obligations three times a year Ex 23:14. Solomon rebuilt the cities of Hazor, Megiddo and Gezer identified by archeology and associated with Pharaoh Shishak 945–924 BC v15,16; 14:25,26.

9:26-28 Solomon established lucrative sea trade from Ezion Geber on the north point of the Red Sea to Ophir (Arabia, east Africa) with Hiram, king of Tyre, compatriot of David 1Kin 5:1.

10:1-13 **The Queen of Sheba** came to investigate his wisdom and understanding and was amazed at his ability. She recognized his knowledge was due to his relationship with the LORD. God's love for Israel had made him king to maintain justice and righteousness v2,9. The reports were not even half the evidence she saw. Solomon gave the queen all she desired.

10:14-23 **Solomon's Splendor** He increased in possessions and success becoming greater in riches and wisdom v23.

Solomon's Failure

Having completed his building projects and established peace the last ten years of his reign were of decline. Achieving so much in wealth, fame and prominence his pride and self-importance led him to forget the One who had given him all things. While Song of Songs portrayed his early love and Proverbs revealed his wisdom Ecclesiastes showed his frustration with life as he turned away from God.

Four requirements were given for kings which Solomon failed to keep –

10:24,25 **Wealth** Solomon accumulated large wealth Deu 17:17.

10:26-29 **Possessions** He acquired great numbers of horses from Egypt Deu 17:16.

11:1-4 **Foreign Compromise** He took many wives from foreign nations Deu 17:17; Neh 13:26.

11:5,6 **Loss of 'first love'** He did not read God's Word to revere the LORD Deu 17:18-20. Solomon demonstrated the folly of not applying the spiritual disciplines of growth - he drifted into the ways of the world Acts 2:42-47; Rev 2:4,5.

11:7,8 **High Places** These local places of worship allowed the introduction of foreign gods. Solomon's involvement with these practices shows the danger of wrong associations.

High Places - these hilltop altars scattered throughout the land were not under the control of the Temple worship in Jerusalem and allowed heathen practices to be introduced. They were a great offence because they included physical idols along side of the worship of the Most High God who is Eternal Spirit.

THE KINGDOM DIVIDED
11:9-40 **The LORD'S Anger** The LORD became angry with Solomon and told him that after his death ten of the twelve tribes would be taken from him v11. As a result of Solomon's disobedience adversaries rose up to challenge his authority v14,23. Jeroboam, one of his capable officials was given a prophetic word by Ahijah the prophet about the transfer of the kingdom v26.

11:41-43 Solomon died at 59 years of age.

SUMMARY
The United Kingdom In 120 years God gave Israel three kings in succession to demonstrate the frailty of human leadership -
• Saul met the standard of the world but failed 1Sam 9:2; 15:10,11
• David met the standard of God and the LORD gave him victory wherever he went 1Sam 13:14; 16:7; 2Sam 8:6
• Solomon was the wisest king, wealthy and famous but became foolish towards God and lost ten tribes of the kingdom 11:9-13.
The Divided Kingdom As a result of Solomon's unfaithfulness the kingdom was divided. With his death ten tribes in the north were ruled by Jeroboam, Solomon's exiled official and took the name of Israel (sometimes known as Ephraim, the most influential tribe) 11:31. The LORD allowed the southern tribe of Judah and Benjamin to remain with Solomon's son Rehoboam for the sake of David and for the royal line of kings 1Kin 11:36; 2Sam 7:16 to continue to Jesus Lk 1:32,32. The future glory of the royal line of David is foreshadowed in the end time 11:39; Rev 5:5; 19:15,16.
The division of the kingdom meant mutual hostility and rivalry between north and south. The neighboring nations (Philistia, Aram, Ammon and Moab) broke free of Israel's domination, no longer paying tribute and in time became oppressors. Israel lost control of the trade routes.
Northern Kingdom (Israel) The ten tribes contained 75% of the people – the land area was three times greater than the south and included the

Jordan Valley. However the people immediately turned away from the LORD and brought about their own downfall. As conduct worsened the great miracle-working prophets Elijah and Elisha were raised by God to demonstrate God's sovereignty over idols and to foretell judgment.

There were 9 different dynasties with 19 kings all of whom were unfaithful (did evil in the eyes of the LORD). After 208 years of disobedience Israel was conquered by Assyria in 722 BC. The people were dispersed among the nations (the Diaspora). God's mercy is great but his judgment is sure.

Southern Kingdom (Judah) David's tribe of Judah was the largest individual tribe and incorporated Benjamin. The nation was land locked but had the capital of Jerusalem and the Temple. Many Levites and people from other tribes defected to Jerusalem because of the Temple. This meant that a remnant of every tribe remained with Judah 2Chr 11:13-17. Even so they only represented 25% of the people. There were 20 southern kings all of the royal line of Judah of whom 8 were faithful to the LORD. Judah existed for a further 136 years (a total of 344 years) and despite a number of short-lived reforms they were taken into captivity by Babylon in 586 BC. A remnant returned to Jerusalem after 70 years in exile. They were known from then as Jews.

Period At the time of Israel's entry to Canaan 1400–1100 BC the local people lived in a loose confederacy of city-states Jos 10:3,5; 11:1-5 under the general influence of Egypt. Throughout the reigns of David and Solomon 1010–930 BC there was a period of weakness in the north as the dominant Babylonians contested with other nations and finally succumbed to the New Assyrian Empire which became dominant from 900–612 BC.

Under the kings of the Divided Kingdom there was regular conflict between Egypt and Assyria involving Israel until the fall of Samaria 722 BC. Nineveh the capital of Assyria fell to Babylon 612 BC.

Judah fell to Babylon 586 BC. In the remainder of the Books of Kings few details are given except where the focus is on the relationship of the kings and the people with God.

The Bible record from 1Kin 12:1 to 2 Kin 17:41 describes the north and south kingdoms roughly in chronological order. In the following sections the events of the two kingdoms are set out on consecutive pages to provide continuity within each kingdom with cross reference to the text.

Kings of Judah 930–850 BC

Rehoboam 930 BC – 17 years. Son of Solomon
12:1-24 **Ten Tribes Rebelled** After the death of Solomon his son Rehoboam went to Shechem to be made king over all Israel. The people asked for relief from Solomon's excessive tax burden required to fund his massive projects. His older advisers agreed but he went with his young colleagues who suggested harsher burdens. As a result the ten northern tribes rebelled under the leadership of Jeroboam retaining the name of Israel v20. Rehoboam became king over the southern kingdom. Benjamin remained with Judah. Many from the northern tribes particularly Levites moved to Jerusalem because of the Temple worship. Rehoboam prepared for war but was warned not to proceed as this division was God's doing as prophesied v24; 11:31. 12:25

14:21-31 Rehoboam despite his heritage did evil in God's sight worse than Jeroboam even following the practices and idol's of the heathen nations. Shishak king of Egypt 945-924 BC who had collaborated with Solomon 9:16 invaded Jerusalem and took much of the Temple and Palace treasury. This event is recorded among his conquests on the temple in Thebes 925 BC.

Abijah 913 BC – 3 years. (18th year of Jeroboam)
15:1-8 Abijah, son of Rehoboam, followed the evil ways of his father Rehoboam. Yet God continued the royal line of David. War remained between Judah and Israel.

Asa 910 BC – 41 years. Son of Abijah (20th year of Jeroboam)
15:9-24 Asa was a good king - followed faithfully in the ways of David. He began a series of reforms even deposing his evil grandmother. His heart was fully committed to the LORD. When Baasha king of Israel blockaded the border of Judah Asa purchased a treaty with Aram (Syria) allowing the blockade to be broken 2Chr 14:1 to 16:14.

Jehoshaphat 873 BC – 25 years. (4th year of Ahab)
15:24 Jehoshaphat, son of Asa was a good king. 15:25
22:41-50 He continued to tolerate the high places of Solomon.
He made peace with Ahab, evil king of Israel which almost cost him his life v1-40; 2Chr 17:1 to 20:37. 22:51

Kings of Israel 930–885 BC

Jeroboam 1 930 BC – 22 years. Son of Nebat
12:25-33 **The Separate Kingdom of Israel** One of Solomon's capable officials 11:28 who rebelled and fled to Egypt returned on the death of Solomon. He led the revolt against Solomon's son Rehoboam uniting the ten northern tribes into a new kingdom of Israel with the capital at Shechem. Jeroboam was God's choice in order to show the people once again the result of living independent of God and his commandments 11:29-39. Despite God's promises he immediately set up idol worship with golden calves at Bethel and at Dan in northern Israel to discourage the people from returning to Jerusalem and the Temple for regular worship v28. This led to other evil practices contrary to the Word of God demonstrating once again that skill and natural ability are not sufficient to rule.
13:1 to 14:20 A man of God from Judah under instruction from God condemned the practices of Jeroboam but paid with his life due to disobedience. The altar was split and Jeroboam's arm was shriveled. This was a severe warning to Jeroboam after the initial instructions and great promises given to him by God 11:31-39 but he refused to take heed. Ahijah the prophet who announced his ascendancy also forecast disaster on the house of Jeroboam including the death of his son 14:4,5,10. 14:21

Nadab 910 BC – 2 years. Son of Jeroboam (2nd year of Asa)
15:25-32 Nadab did evil as his father had. He was executed in battle by Baasha, a countryman who assassinated his whole family and reigned in his place v29; 14:10.

Baasha 909 BC – 24 years. Son of Ahijah (3rd year of Asa)
15:33 to 16:7 Baasha did evil before being judged and replaced by his son.

Elah 886 BC – 2 years. Son of Baasha (26th year of Asa)
16:8-10 Elah was executed by Zimri one of his officials.

Zimri 885 BC - 7 days. An official (27th year of Asa)
16:11-20 Zimri executed the whole family of Baasha then was forced to commit suicide.

Special Prophet to Israel – Elijah 874-852 BC - 22 years

17:1-6 **Elijah Commissioned** With the appearance of evil Ahab in Israel God raised up a special miracle-working prophet as an angel of judgment to confront him. **Elijah** the Tishbite was called to serve in Israel as a prophet during the reign of Ahab and Ahaziah over twenty-two years.

Elijah declared there would be no rain except at his word v1.

Despite the series of evil kings Elijah recognized that Israel (including Judah) remained the chosen domain and people of God and would always be so! God provided food and water for Elijah during the three years of drought.

17:7-24 **The Widow from Zarephath** When food ran out God provided a poor widow with food and water for Elijah as well as for herself and child. We may always depend on God to provide all our needs Phil 4:19. When the widow's son died he was miraculously brought back to life confirming Elijah's authority.

18:1-15 **A Devout Believer** When God told Elijah that the end of the drought was due he advised Obadiah the palace manager to summons Ahab. Obadiah required Elijah's reassurance before he would comply.

18:16-46 **Fire From Heaven** Elijah called the false prophets to present a sacrifice on Mt Carmel to confirm the superiority of God. *How long will you waver between two opinions? v21.* When the prophets failed to receive an answer Elijah repaired the altar calling fire from God obtaining a rousing response – *The LORD he is God! v39.* He executed the prophets.

Elijah went to the top of Carmel to wait for rain to come. He prayed seven times – we can be sure God answers persistent prayer. We can stand before the throne of God just as Elijah did, with all our weaknesses, righteous because of the death of Jesus and pray earnest, effective prayers Jas 5:15-18. Elijah ran down the hill ahead of Ahab. Still Ahab did not submit to God.

Jezreel was located 30 km north of Samaria near Mt Carmel.

Kings of Israel 885-883 BC

Omri 885 BC – 12 years. A commander (31st year of Asa)
16:21-28 Omri was appointed king by popular demand. He relocated the capital of Israel from Shechem some 10 km northwest to Samaria. He was an evil king (recorded on the Moabite Stone). 16:29
Ahab 874 BC – 22 years. Son of Omri (38th year of Asa)
16:29-34 After six evil kings in Israel over 56 years Ahab son of Omri did more evil than any of those before him. He retained the idols of Jehoboam, and married Jezebel the evil daughter of the king of Sidon. She killed the LORD's prophets, set up 400 evil prophets and introduced worship of Baal a heathen idol. As Ahab brought Israel to the lowest point in turning from God the great prophet Elijah was raised up to challenge him. 17:1
20:1-43 **War With Aram** The northern neighbor of Israel, Aram (Syria) provided a buffer against the might of the expanding Assyrian Empire. However as they prospered they began to oppress Israel.
Ben-Hadad II king of Aram 860-841 BC besieged Samaria and demanded tribute. In his compassion and patience God intervened to encourage Israel to repent. With guidance from a man of God Ahab managed to confront and defeat Aram. The next year Aram returned to fight Israel on the plain - they doubted God's previous intervention - again with God's help Israel was victorious. Ahab foolishly released Ben-Hadad with a treaty contrary to God's request, an act his son would regret. The dedication of those who serve God is contrasted with those who do not v35, 42.
21:1-29 **Naboth's Vineyard** Ahab wanted the vineyard of one of the locals. It was Naboth's duty to preserve his inheritance. Jezebel arranged to have him killed. Elijah pronounced judgment on Ahab, Jezebel and his family for this deed. However because of Ahab's sorrow it was delayed.

Elijah 874-852 BC - 22 years (continued)

19:1-15 **Elijah's Retreat - the still small voice** When Jezebel pursued him Elijah escaped to Beersheba in the southern desert. He was distressed by the conflict. Strengthened by food he went on to Horeb (Mt Sinai) where **God spoke to him**, not in a great wind, earthquake or fire, but as God usually speaks, in a gentle whisper - we must practice listening! We may never feel alone when we walk with the LORD. Elijah revealed the source of his power. He was like us subject to fear yet able to accomplish great things through faith when submitted to God 2Cor 12:9.

19:15-21 Elijah was given further ministry to perform – anointing Hazael king of Aram, anointing Jehu king over Israel and the calling and anointing of Elisha his successor. God is involved in the affairs of mankind and always has work to do. Elisha responded immediately to the call v21. 20:1

Kings of Israel 883-853 BC

22:1-28 **Micaiah's Prophecy** Conflict remained between Judah and Israel for 60 years. Near the end of Ahab's reign Jehoshapat visited him and agreed to join in battle to recover the town of Ramoth Gilead. They obtained favorable advice from the false prophets but the one prophet of the LORD foretold disaster. Micaiah was put in prison till they returned.

22:29-40 **Death of Ahab** In the ensuing battle Ahab was killed by a random arrow. The prophetic words spoken against him were fulfilled. Jehoshaphat barely escaped with his life.

The ivory palace built by Ahab has been discovered v39. 22:41

Ahaziah 853 BC – 2 years. Son of Ahab (17th year of Jehoshaphat)

22:51-53 Ahaziah was an evil king.

End of the Book of 1Kings

Special Prophet to Israel – Elisha 852-798 BC - 54 years

2:1-18 **Elisha Commissioned** A second miracle-working prophet succeeded Elijah in Israel during the reigns of Joram, Jehu, Jehoahaz and Jehoash. He prophesied over 54 years.

When the time came for Elijah to depart he tried to dissuade Elisha three times but he was determined to follow to the end. Elijah used his cloak to part the waters of the Jordan. Elisha asked for a double portion of his spirit v9. Then Elijah was whisked away in a horse-drawn chariot of fire in a whirlwind. Elisha picked up Elijah's cloak and parted the Jordan showing that his master's spirit had indeed fallen on him. This was recognized by the watching company of prophets. Our faith is often tested to see our fortitude and persistence. The prophets searched for Elijah in vain.

2:19-25 Elisha purified local water and caused the punishment of some jeering youths.   3:1

4:1-7 **The Widow's Oil** The wife of a deceased prophet was in debt and asked Elisha for help. He told her to fill all the bottles she could find with the little oil she had. She sold the oil to provide for her family. When we commit what we have to the LORD he is able to use it to achieve his purposes Mt 14:17-21.

4:8-37 **A Son Restored** A woman provided lodging for Elisha as he passed by. He foretold that she would have a son. The son subsequently died so Elisha prayed and brought him back to life.

4:38-44 **Feeding the Prophets** Elisha purified a pot of poison stew and fed a hundred people with a gift of bread.

2 Kings

Introduction – The Book of 2 Kings records continuing decline of the people leading to the demise of both Israel and Judah.
Theme - Ultimate Failure of the kingdoms of the world – shown by demise of the divided kingdom of Israel Rev 11:15.
Period - Death of Ahab to the exile of Judah - some 266 years.

Kings of Israel 852-841 BC

1:1-18 Ahaziah was injured and sought advice from a foreign idol. Elijah anticipated this and foretold that he would not recover. Soldiers sent to arrest Elijah were consumed by fire until he agreed to go with them. The king died of his injury as predicted.   2:1

Joram 852 BC – 12 years. (18th year of Jehoshaphat)
3:1–27 **Moab Rebelled** When Ahab died Mesha king of Moab rebelled and refused to pay tribute. Joram, son of Ahab enlisted the support of Jehoshaphat king of Judah and the king of Edom to invade Moab. When out of water they sought the help of Elisha who only responded out of respect for the king of Judah v14. He gave them a battle plan involving water ditches miraculously filled to reflect the glare to look like blood. Moab thought Israel was already slain so came into a trap. The towns of Moab were destroyed and the army routed. When the king sacrificed his son Israel withdrew in disgust.   4:1
6:24 to 7:20 **Steps of Faith - Samaria delivered** Ben-Hadad II king of Aram again besieged Samaria after being foolishly released by Ahab causing great distress 1Kin 20:42. Elisha foretold that food would be plentiful by tomorrow. An officer who did not believe lost his life. God led four lepers to step out in faith, leaving the relative comfort of the city gate and going to the enemy camp at dusk. As they set out the LORD responded by causing the sound of a great army to pass through the camp resulting in the Arameans fleeing to their country leaving all behind. Despite the doubts of Joram they were miraculously delivered.

Elisha 852-798 BC - 54 years (continued)

5:1-27 **Healed of Leprosy** Naaman commander of the army of Aram had leprosy and was led to go to the prophet in Israel to be healed as a result of the witness of a young girl. How important is it to tell what we know about Jesus! Acts 1:8. Naaman went expecting a dramatic healing but was told by Elisha to wash seven times in the Jordan River. When he agreed he was healed and adopted the worship of Israel's (Elisha's) God. Gehazi sought to make gain from the event and became leprous. The healing of this foreign commander is recorded to emphasis the need for faith in God's people.

6:1-7 **An Axe-head Floated** God will help us in all circumstances.

6:8-23 **The Army With Us** Ben-Hadad II of Aram remained at war with Joram of Israel but his attacks were always anticipated by Elisha. When finally encircled by the enemy Elisha revealed to his servant - *those who are with us are more than those who are with them v16.* We need to have our spiritual eyes open to see that God is always on our side. Elisha led the blinded army into captivity and then released them thereby stalling further attacks.   6:24

Kings of Israel 841-798 BC

The lepers are a great example for all who are willing to assess a situation and step out in faith. God continued to provide prophets and guidance in Israel despite their evil actions.

8:1-6 Elisha's friend had her land restored.

8:7-15 **Ben-Hadad Murdered** When Elisha went to Damascus Ben-Hadad sent his officer Hazael to inquire if he would recover from illness. Elisha gave a concealed reply indicating that Hazael would be king of Aram. Hazael subsequently murdered Ben-Hadad and became king. 8:16

9:1-29 **Judgment on Ahab's house** would be administered by Jehu 1Kin 21:21. Elisha sent a prophet to secretly anoint him. Jehu, a commander left the battle at Ramoth Gilead, went to Jezreel and killed Joram on the vineyard of Naboth. He also killed Ahaziah because of his complicity.

9:30 to 10:17 Jehu also arranged the deaths of Jezebel and Ahab's household as foretold by Elijah 1Kin 21:23,24.

Jehu 841 BC – 28 years. (12th year of Joram)

10:18-36 Jehu, son of Jehoshaphat brought the people to Samaria to organize the execution of the prophets of Baal and the destruction of their temple. While he did well in executing judgment on Ahab's family, as king he did not keep the law of the LORD carefully v31. God promised his descendants would rule to the fourth generation. God began to reduce the territory of Israel particularly east of Jordan. Jehu paid tribute to Shalmanessar III king of Assyria in 840 BC (recorded on the Black Obelisk). 11:1

Jehoahaz 814 BC – 17 years. Son of Jehu (23rd year of Joash)

13:1-9 Jehoahaz continued to do evil in the eyes of the LORD as his father had done so Israel was kept under the domination of Hazael king of Aram v3; 8:12. When Jehoahaz appealed to the LORD he provided a deliverer (unknown) v5 so they had peace for a time but still they did not repent and their army was decimated v6. An Aramean stela segment from this time refers to the 'House of David'.

Kings of Judah– 850-797 BC

Jehoram 849 BC – 8 years. Son of Jehoshaphat (5th year of Joram)
  8:16-24 Civil relations developed between Judah and Israel. Jehoram married a daughter of Ahab and followed in his evil ways. God still persevered with Judah for the sake of David and the royal line leading to Jesus. The people of Edom 90 km south, rebelled against Israel and broke free of tribute.

Ahaziah 841 BC - 1 year. Son of Jehoram (12th year of Joram)
  8:25-29 Ahaziah also married into Ahab's family and became an evil king. He supported Joram in war against Hazael of Aram over the disputed city of Ramoth Gilead. When Joram was wounded he returned to Jezreel to recover and was visited by Ahaziah. Both were killed by Jehu.   9:1

Athaliah 841 BC – 6 years. (12th year of Joram)
  11:1-21 When Ahaziah was killed by Jehu his mother, Athaliah destroyed the whole royal family. One son Joash was rescued by his sister and hidden in the Temple for six years. Then the priest Jehoiada arranged a coup with the army and crowned Joash king of Judah. Athaliah was executed.

Joash 836 BC– 40 years. Son of Ahaziah (7th year of Jehu)
  11:17-21 The young Joash was given a copy of the Covenant and committed with the people to be faithful to the LORD.
  12:1-21 **The Temple Repaired** Raised by the priest Jehoiada, Joash was faithful to God. He ordered the offerings be used to repair damage to the Temple. After twenty-three years delay the task was given to civilian workers who completed the work honestly. But the high places were not removed. Hazael king of Aram invaded Judah but withdrew when Joash paid tribute from the Temple. Joash was assassinated by two officials. 13:1

Kings of Israel 753-722 BC

Jehoash 798 BC – 16 years. (37th year of Joash)
13:10–13 Jehoash, son of Jehoahaz did evil.
13:14-21 **Death of Elisha** Elisha became ill and received a visit from Jehoash out of respect. Elisha foretold victory against Aram but as it was not enthusiastically received in faith it would only be partial. Elisha then died. During a raid by Moabites some Israelites were disturbed during a burial. They threw the body into Elisha's tomb and the man came back to life! v21.
13:22-25 When Hazael king of Aram 841-801 BC died his son Ben-Hadad III 807-780 BC succeeded him. Israel gained relief from Aram and recovered captured Israelite cities. 14:1

Jeroboam II 793 BC – 41 years. (15th year of Amaziah)
14:23-29 Jeroboam II, son of Jehoash continued in the evil ways of his forefathers. Yet the LORD gave them some relief from their oppression by the word of Jonah the prophet. 15:1

Zechariah 753 BC – 6 months. (38th year of Azariah)
15:8-12 Zechariah, son of Jeroboam II was assassinated.

Shallum 752 BC - 1 month. (39th year of Azariah)
15:13-16 Shallum, son of Jabesh was assassinated.

Menahem 751 BC – 10 years. (39th year of Azariah)
15:17-22 Menahem, son of Gadi did evil in the eyes of the LORD. As Assyria became more dominant Tiglath-Pileser III king of Assyria 745-727 BC invaded Israel. Menahem extracted the tribute from his own people.

Pekahiah 741 BC – 2 years. (50th year of Azariah)
15:23-26 Pekahiah, son of Menahem was assassinated.

Pekah 740 BC – 20 years. (52nd year of Azariah)
15:27-31 Pekah, son of Remaliah did evil. Tiglath-Pileser III again invaded Israel and took the north region of the country including Gilead *and* Galilee deporting the people to Assyria. Pekah was assassinated by Hosea. 15:32

Kings of Judah 751-696 BC

Amaziah 797 BC – 29 years. Son of Joash (2nd year of Jehoash)
  14:1-22 Amaziah did what was right but continued with the high places. He executed the officials who murdered his father but not the sons. He repossessed an Edomite city. He then foolishly challenged Jehoash king of Israel to war and was defeated. Israel took a heavy toll on Judah destroying the wall of Jerusalem and taking tribute. Amaziah was assassinated.   14:23

Azariah 791 BC – 52 years. Son of Amaziah (27th year of Jeroboam II)
  15:1-7 Azariah (Uzziah) did what was right but also retained the high places. This was compromise with the world. He took the priests duty and contracted leprosy. His son had charge of the land (co-regent). 15:8

Jotham 751 BC – 16 years. Son of Azariah (2nd year of Pekah)
  15:32-38 Jotham did right in the eyes of the LORD but still allowed the high places. He was oppressed by Aram and Israel.

Ahaz 736 BC – 16 years. Son of Jotham (17th year of Pekah)
  16:1-20 Ahaz was evil following the ways of Israel. Rezin king of Aram and Pekah king of Israel besieged Jerusalem but could not defeat it. Ahaz paid tribute to Tiglath-Pileser III king of Assyria to conquer Damascus. In Damascus to meet Tiglath-Pileser Ahaz copied a foreign altar for prominent use in the Temple in Jerusalem. He made many other major changes to the Temple and services contrary to the Word of God.   17:1

Kings of Israel 731-722 BC

Hoshea 731 BC – 9 years. Son of Elah (12th year of Ahaz)

17:1-6 An evil king, Hoshea was a vassal of Shalmaneser V king of Assyria 727-722 BC but he sided with Egypt. Shalmaneser lay siege to Samaria for three years until it finally fell 722 BC (possibly to his son Sargon II 722-705 BC) v6. Hoshea was put in prison, the nobles and leading people of Israel were deported to Mesopotamia and Media.

FALL OF ISRAEL

17:7-23 The northern kingdom of Israel fell to Assyria and the people were dispersed among the nations because all 19 kings were evil and led the people away from God. Many prophets were raised up to repeatedly challenge and warn the people to return to the ways of the LORD as set down in the Covenant with Moses but they refused to respond. Consequently they were scattered, most never to return v23.

17:24-41 People from foreign countries were imported to repopulate Samaria by Assyria to break up the ethnic cohesion. A priest who had been exiled from Samaria was brought to live at Bethel to teach the people how to follow the Levitical worship. People in the various locations worshiped the LORD but also included idols from their own cultures in the high places. They came to bear the name 'Samaritan' v28-33.   18:1

Hezekiah 721 BC – 29 years. Son of Ahaz (3rd year of Hoshea)

18:1-8 **A Good King** Hezekiah did what was right in the eyes of the LORD just as his father David had done v3 – there was no one like him. He introduced real reform, removed the heathen high places, smashed the idols and was successful in breaking the yoke of Assyria and the Philistines. He served the LORD and kept the commands the LORD had given to Moses. He fortified the cities and strengthened the water sources in Jerusalem.

18:9-12 **Fall of Israel** In the 4th year of Hezekiah's reign Samaria was besieged by Shalmaneser king of Assyria and fell in 722 BC. The people of Israel were dispersed leaving Judah exposed to further assault.

18:13-16 **Judah Under Siege** In the 14th year of Hezekiah Sennacherib king of Assyria 705-681 BC captured all the fortified cities of Judah including Lachish 701 BC. Hezekiah paid tribute and so Jerusalem was spared.

18:17-37 **Jerusalem under Siege** Sennacherib's army returned and demanded surrender – *how can the LORD deliver? v35.*

19:1-37 **Power of Prayer** Jerusalem was delivered at the word of Isaiah by miraculous intervention of God *19:20 – 'because you prayed to me'* Is 37:21. We may be confident that God acts on our behalf when we pray to him. God knows all things, plans all things and brings all things to pass 19:20-34.This event is recorded on Sennacherib's Prism - he returned to Nineveh and was executed by his two sons 681 BC 19:37.

20:1-21 **Hezekiah's Increase in Life** When Hezekiah became ill he prayed for longer life and was granted fifteen years. A sign was given that the shadow recede ten steps. Envoys came from Babylon to inquire about the healing and rather than hearing praise because of God's kindness and miraculous healing they were shown Hezekiah's wealth. Isaiah foretold that Judah's wealth would be carried off to Babylon.

While Hezekiah was a good king his extra fifteen years were not productive as he failed to give glory to God for his healing and he bore an evil son. 21:1

Kings of Judah 696-598 BC

Manasseh 693 BC – 55 years. Son of Hezekiah
21:1-18 Manasseh born to Hezekiah in his extra years was evil. He rebuilt the high places and followed the practices of the nations. God had promised Israel so much. Manasseh was the personification of all the evil they had done and was responsible for shedding much innocent blood. When Manasseh was taken into captivity by Assyria he repented so God allowed him to return to Jerusalem where he introduced reforms 2Chr 33:11-20.

Amon 639 BC – 1 year. Son of Manasseh
21:19-26 Amonn did evil as his father and was assassinated.

Josiah 639 BC – 31 years. Son of Amon
22:1-20 **The Book of the Law** Josiah was a good king who arranged reforms and repairs to the Temple. Hilkiah the high priest found the Book of the Law in the Temple which had been abandoned Jos 1:8. When the young Josiah heard the words of the Book of the Law he was devastated. He was advised that although Jerusalem would be punished for turning away from the Covenant yet because his heart was responsive and he humbled himself before the LORD he would be spared.
23:1-28 **The Covenant Renewed** Josiah called together the people of Judah and read to them all the words of the Book of the Covenant. They then pledged themselves to keep the Covenant. Josiah ordered all heathen idols be removed from the Temple. He destroyed all the high places built by Solomon in Judah and by Jeroboam in Bethel and Samaria. They celebrated the Passover with great enthusiasm v21; 2Chr 35;1-19.
23:29,30 Assyria was waning in power under threat from Babylon. Nineveh capital of Assyria fell to Nabopolassar 626-606 BC in 612 BC. Josiah was killed at Megiddo in a foolish conflict with Neco king of Egypt 609-593 BC who went to Carchemish in 609 BC to aid Assyria 2Chro 35:20.

Jehoahaz 609 BC – 3 months. Son of Josiah
23:31-35 Jehoahaz did evil in the eyes of the LORD and was deported in chains to Egypt by Neco where he died. Tribute was imposed on Judah.

Kings of Judah 598-586 BC

Jehoiakim 608 BC – 11 years. Son of Josiah

23:36 to 24:7 Jehoiakim (Eliakim) was appointed vassal king of Judah by Neco in 608 BC. In 605 BC Nebuchadrezzar II 605-562 BC conquered Carchemish and dominated from Egypt to the Euphrates. He invaded Jerusalem taking evil Jehoiakim and many officials, including Daniel to Babylon. This was the beginning of the desolation of Judah foretold Jer 25:11,12.

Jehoiachin 598 BC – 3 months. Son of Jehoiakim

24:8-17 Nebuchadnezzar returned to lay siege on Jerusalem and in 597 BC he took evil Jehoiachin to Babylon along with many nobles, officials, military and craftsmen including Ezekiel.

Zedekiah 597 BC – 11 years. Uncle of Jehohiachin

24:18 to 25:21 Zedekiah did evil in the eyes of the LORD. He also rebelled against Babylon.

25:1-21 **Fall of Jerusalem** After a two year siege Nebuchadnezzar broke down the walls of the city and set fire to the Temple in 586 BC. The king and the remaining officials were exiled to Babylon with only the poor left.

So Judah went into captivity, away from her land v21.

25:22-26 **Gedaliah** 586 BC was appointed governor over Jerusalem and encouraged the remaining people to settle down and be good citizens as advised by Jeremiah Jer 42:9-12. But he was assassinated along with the Babylonian representatives by some truant army officers. The remaining people fled to Egypt for fear of reprisal by Babylon.

25:27-30 Jehoiachin was eventually released from prison in Babylon and shown kindness because of good behavior.

FALL OF JUDAH 2Chr 36:15-23

The fall of Jerusalem marked the end of Judah and Israel as nations and the end of the Monarchy. The chosen people lost their freedom, city, Temple and nationhood.

There were 20 southern kings all of the royal line of Judah of whom 8 were faithful to the LORD. The reason for the fall of Israel and Judah was that the people had ignored and mocked God's messengers despised his Word and scoffed at his warnings until the LORD was aroused against his people and there was no remedy Hos 8:4.

A remnant would return to Jerusalem after 70 years in exile. They were known from then as Jews and their land as Judea.

Moses foretold failure of the nation of Israel. He also explained the way of repentance and restoration of a remnant Deu 4:25-31.

World Leaders at the Time of the Divided Kingdoms		
Assyrian BC	**Neo-Babylonian** BC	**Medo-Persian** BC
Assur-nasirpal II 883-859	Nabopolassar 626-606	Cyrus II 559-530
Shalmaneser III 858-824	Nebuchadrezzar II 605-562	*Governor – Darius 539
Shamshi-Adad V 823-811	*Carchemish – Egypt 605	Cambyses II 530-522
Adad-niari III 810-783	*Ashkelon, Judah 599	Smerdis 522
Shalmaneser IV 782-773	*Jerusalem 587	Darius I 522-486
Assur-dan III 772-755	Evil-Merodach 562-560	Ahasureus 486-465
Assur-nirari V 754-745	Nergal-Sharezer 560-556	*Xerxes I, Salamis 480
Tiglath-Pileser III 745-727	Labashi-Marduk 556	*Esther 479
Shalmaneser V 727-722	Nabonidus 556-539	Artaxerxes 465-424
Sargon II 722-705	Belshazzar 553-539	Sogdianus 425
Sennacherib 705-681	*Fall of Babylon 539	Xerxes II 424-423
Esarhaddon 681-699		Daruis II 424-404
Ashurbanipal 669-627		Darius III 336-330
*Fall of Nineveh 612		

1 Chronicles

Introduction – The two Books of Chronicles were likely one and possibly compiled by the same author as Ezra and Nehemiah (compare 2Chr 36:22,23 and Ezr 1:1-3). They were written during or after the exile when the Persians conquered Babylon and allowed captive people to return to their homeland.

The Chronicles provide a review of the history of Israel over the period of the kings to the fall of Jerusalem and the release of the exiled people.

Author – Ezra the reformer, priest and scribe complied this review of the Monarchy taken from the official records of the kings and recorders 1Ch 29:29; 2Chr 16:11 for the benefit of the returning exiles around 460 BC.

Period – A genealogy from the beginning, including the reign of the kings from Saul 1150 BC to the exile of Judah 586 BC a period of some 564 years.

Theme -The Household of God During the exile in Babylon the people were demoralized Ps 137. They had lost their homeland and monarchy. They had no political freedom and little hope for a national future. The purpose of Chronicles was to review the history of Israel to remind the exiles of their heritage and that **they were still the chosen people of God.** The prophets Isaiah, Jeremiah, Ezekiel and Daniel foretold the return of a remnant to the Promised Land with the restoration of Jerusalem and the Temple. They also foretold the coming of a king of the royal line of David. These prophecies confirmed the Covenant God made with David - *I will set him over my house and my kingdom forever; his throne will be established forever 17:11-14.* This will be fulfilled at the Second Coming of Jesus Christ.

The record conforms with the Books of Kings but is more selective and tends to portray the good side of the history. The intention was to show the people that when they honored God and followed his commandments they prospered. When they turned away from God they were disciplined. The Monarchy and Temple were human innovations. God used them as shadows to confirm the reality that came into being with Jesus.

1Chronicles Ten chapters give a genealogy of the patriarchs and twelve tribes of Israel from Adam through the kings to the remnant who returned from captivity. After the death of Saul the reign of David focuses on his faithfulness to God and his desire to build the Temple.

2Chronicles The reign of Solomon is described followed by the decline of the Southern Kingdom of Judah to the fall of Jerusalem, the captivity and the announcement of the return from exile. The faithful acts of the kings of the royal line of Judah are described with the attempts at reforms. The Northern Kingdom of Israel is only mentioned in connection with Judah as all of their kings were evil.

The Genealogies of the Patriarchs and People of Israel
1:1-54 Adam through Noah to Abraham.

2:1-55 The Tribes of Israel (twelve sons of Jacob).

3:1-24 **David and the Kings of Judah** – all 20 kings of Judah after Solomon were of the royal line of David.

4:1 to 8:40 **The Descendants of Israel** up to the time of the Captivity.

9:1-34 **The Exiles who returned to Jerusalem** There were many records of genealogies and events of the Israelite kings and people compiled and kept by the official recorders, the priests and the scribes v1. The people went to great length to maintain the purity of their lineage - from Adam to Jesus.

9:35 to 10:14 **Saul First King of Israel** His life was summarized in a statement of his unfaithfulness to God 10:13.

DAVID APPOINTED KING OVER ISRAEL 2Sam 5:1-5
11:1-3 The detailed record starts with all Israel unified under David.

11:4-9 **Jerusalem Conquered** David's first act was to take the hillside Jebusite city of Jerusalem and establish it as Zion, the City of David, capital of Israel. David's success was recognized as being due to the favor of the LORD 2Sam 5:10-12.

11:10 to 12:40 David was supported by mighty men many of whom were with him in his flight from Saul and when he was king in Hebron 12:23.

The Ark brought to Jerusalem 2Sam 6:1-23.

13:1-14 David's next significant act was to bring the Ark of the LORD to Jerusalem. This established the city as the center of worship as well as the political capital. The irreverent act of Uzzah brought death, fear and delay. Desire for intimacy with God must be accompanied by respect and awe v12.

14:1-17 David built a palace and secured the kingdom. He subdued the Philistines after inquiring of the LORD v14,16.

15:1-29 Following three months of delay caused by the death of Uzzah David again proceeded to bring the Ark to Jerusalem. He pitched a tent *v1* – the original Tabernacle by this time was located at Gibeon 16:39. He made sure of the correct method for transporting the Ark according to Num 4:4-15. Previously they had not inquired of the LORD v15.

16:1-6 He presented offerings and reinstated the daily service of the Levites under Asaph to make petition, to give thanks and to praise God as instructed in the Book of the Law Lev 23:2.

16:7-36 **David's Thanksgiving Psalm** at the return of the Ark.

16:36-43 Worship continued at the Tabernacle and altar at Gibeon under the priest Zadok.

Gibeon where Joshua gained a victory when Israel first entered Canaan. It became a place of celebration Jos 10:12-14.

AN ETERNAL KINGDOM - God's Promise to David

17:1-15 David wanted to build a house for the Ark of the LORD. God told Nathan to rebuke the Temple concept v5. David was told *I declare to you that the LORD will build a house for you v10.* The Lord would make his name great and raise up an offspring whose kingdom would be everlasting – this promise was fulfilled in Jesus – we are his house Heb 3:6. The Temple was permitted as a shadow of things to come.

17:16-27 **David's Prayer of Thanksgiving** for God's promise of an eternal kingdom with people of all nations 2Sam 7:18-29.

David's Victories 2Sam 8:1-14

18:1-17 The LORD gave David victory everywhere he went David's success was as a result of his relationship with God - an example for us to follow. All God's blessings are promised to those who obey Eph 1:3. Conversely our frustrations are because of our reluctance to honor God and give him first place in our lives Deu 28:1-68.

Among the kings officials were recorders and secretaries v14-17.

19:1-19 **Conflict with Ammon** 2Sam 10:1-19 A kind act by David was turned to war.

20:1-3 **Ammon Subdued** David's great sin against Bathsheba, Uriah and the LORD is not mentioned 2Sam 11:1-27 to 12:31. It occurred during the battle of Rabbah. The seven consequences of his sin are also omitted 2Sam 13:1 to 18:33.

20:4-8 There was regular conflict with the Philistines who were subdued by David.

The Site of the Temple 2Sam 24:1-25

21:1-17 A census was taken which brought a plague. It was due to pride and self-dependence v3. David was given three options and chose to fall into the hands of God v12. The plague was stopped.

21:18-30 The LORD told David to build an altar on the threshing floor of Araunah the Jebusite where the plague stopped v18. David bought the land, built an altar and made an offering to God. Do not offer to the LORD what costs us nothing v24. This site is the historic Mt Moriah where Abraham was called to offer his son, Isaac and where Solomon would build the Temple 2Sam 5:6-10; 2Chr 3:1. It was also where David took Goliath's head 1Sam 17:54. The Dome of the Rock now stands there. This showed the fear and reverence David had for God v30.

Preparing for Building the Temple

22:1-19 Just as the request for a king did not come from God neither did the request for a Temple 17:6. While God allowed the building of the Temple it was no longer required when Jesus came. The Temple was destroyed finally in AD 70. We are now God's temple of the Holy Spirit 1Cor 3:16 and the house that God is building 1Pet 2:5.

Although told he could not build the Temple David understood that his son Solomon would 22:9,10; 2Sam 7:13. He began extensive preparations for the Temple and gave detailed instructions to Solomon. *Now devote your heart and soul to seeking the LORD your God v19.* This was wise advice from which Solomon departed in his later years resulting in the dividing of the earthly kingdom.

23:1 to 26:32 David's organization included the Temple service, divisions of the priests, the Temple singers, the ministry of prophecy and singing, the gatekeepers, treasurers, administrators, judges and other officials.

27:1-34 The army divisions, officers and overseers.

28:1-21 David's final charge for them to build the Temple.

The Promise – *I will establish his kingdom forever if he is unswerving in carrying out my commands and laws, as is being done at this time v7.* **The Condition** – *The LORD searches every heart and understands every motive behind the thoughts. If you seek him, he will be found by you v9.*

It is the same today – God reveals himself to you when you genuinely seek him with all your whole heart Jer 29:13,14.

The Holy Spirit inspired the plans for the Temple in the mind of David as he did for the Tabernacle with Moses. He wrote down all that the LORD had instructed him v12.

29:1-9 The source of finance for the Temple was outlined.

29:10-20 **David's Prayer of Thanksgiving** contains many great truths about the nature and character of God -

• God is eternal – from everlasting to everlasting v10

• all greatness, power, glory, majesty and splendor are his because everything in heaven and earth is his - by right of creation and redemption v11

• God's kingdom will remain when all else is finished and he is exalted as head over all v11

• wealth and honor come from him – the ruler of all things v12

• in his hands are strength and power to exalt v12

• everything comes from him and we give to him only what comes from his hand v14

• we are aliens, life is short, our days are like shadows, without hope v15. God tests the heart and is pleased with integrity v17

• our true approach to God is with reverence and praise v20.

Solomon Acknowledged as King 970-930 BC – 40 years

29:21-30 David died aged 70 after 40 years of rule. Records were kept by Samuel, Nathan and Gad as well as the official recorders. Solomon was appointed king at 19 years of age and Zadok became priest.

2 Chronicles

Introduction – The royal line of David is followed from the reign of Solomon through the decline of the Southern Kingdom of Judah to the fall of Jerusalem and the captivity in Babylon, over some 384 years. The announcement of the return from exile is given. The faithful acts of the kings of the royal line of Judah are described with the attempts at reforms. The Northern Kingdom of Israel is only mentioned in connection with Judah as all of their kings were evil.

Period - From the reign of Solomon 970 BC to the exile of Judah 586 BC a period of 384 years.

Theme - Decline, Failure and Captivity Despite the continuing message of the prophets the kings and people would not commit themselves to God.

SOLOMON SECURED AS KING 970-930 BC – 40 years

1:1-12 **Wisdom to Rule** Solomon came to a peaceful reign. He chose to celebrate his kingship at the high place at Gibeon where the Tabernacle and bronze altar were located rather than the location of the Ark in Jerusalem. *The LORD appeared to Solomon* and gave him a request. He chose a discerning heart to govern the people v5. This pleased God who promised him riches and honor as well 1Kin 3:1-15

1:13-17 From the start, Solomon began to accumulate wealth.

BUILDING THE TEMPLE 1Kin 6:1-38

2:1-18 Solomon conscripted the foreigners in Israel as workers. Hiram king of Tyre agreed to supply timber and skilled supervisors for the work.

3:1-17 **The Temple** was 27 m long x 9 m wide x 13.5 m high 1Kin 6:2,3 – designed to the proportions of the Tabernacle but twice the size (14 x 4.6 x 5 m). It was begun in the fourth year of Solomon's reign 966 BC, took seven years to build and was dedicated in 959 BC v38. The Most Holy Place was in the western end adorned by two sculptured cherubim and separated from the Holy Place by a curtain. The Temple was located on Mt Moriah, the site purchased by his father 2Sam 24:18-25.

4:1-22 **Temple Furnishings** Everything was modeled after the original Tabernacle on a more lavish scale Ex 25:8,9.

5:1-14 **They brought up the Ark of the LORD's Covenant from Zion the City of David** 1Kin 8:4. Zion was less than one km from the site of the Temple. **God revealed his glory,** so intense that the priests could not perform their service v14.

6:1-11 **Solomon's Psalm of Praise** 1Kin 8:12-21.

6:12-42 **Prayer of Dedication** 1Kin 8:22-61.

7:1-10 **Dedication of the Temple** 1Kin 8:62-66.

7:11-22 **The LORD Appeared** 1Kin 9:1-9.

Solomon's Fame

8:1-18 **Solomon's Business Activities** 1Kin 9:10-28.

9:1-12 **Queen of Sheba** 1Kin 10:1-13.

9:13-31 **Solomon's Splendor** 1Kin 10:14-29.

Solomon's Failure 1Kin 11:1-8 There is no mention of Solomon's latter years of decline. Only the more positive events were repeated for the encouragement of the exiles.

THE DIVIDED KINGDOM 1Kin 11:9-13

Because of Solomon's ultimate unfaithfulness the LORD removed ten of the twelve tribes from him 1Kin 11:31,32.

10:1-19 **Rehoboam** 930 BC – 17 years. Solomon's son Rehoboam refused to reduce the tax burden and the people rebelled. Ten tribes formed the northern kingdom of Israel under Jeroboam one of Solomon's capable officials 1Kin:12:20. Rehoboam ruled the southern kingdom of Judah. Benjamin remained with Judah and many people including the Levites relocated to Jerusalem because of the Temple worship 11:13,14.

11:1-23 Rehoboam was warned not to make war with Israel so he fortified the cities of Judah. Jeroboam promoted heathen worship in Israel.

12:1-16 When Rehoboam soon abandoned the Law of the LORD Shishak king of Egypt 945-924 BC who had collaborated with Solomon invaded Jerusalem and took much of the Temple and Palace treasury amassed by Solomon (recorded in Egypt among his conquests 925 BC) 1Kin 14:21-31.

When the leaders humbled themselves the city was spared v6-8.

13:1-22 **Abijah** 913 BC – 3 years. Conflict with Israel continued. Although Abijah was not wholehearted in following God they had a form of commitment. God delivered Judah over Israel because they continued to observed the requirements of the LORD during his reign 1Kin 15:1-8.

***14:1-8* Asa** 910 BC – 41 years. Asa was a good king - his heart was fully committed to the LORD all his life. He brought reform to Judah removing the high places, symbols and locations of heathen worship. The high places were particularly offensive because they allowed idols and heathen practices to be included beside the worship of God 1Kin 15:9-24.

***14:9-15* Do not let man prevail against you** Judah was at peace for ten years. When invaded by the Cushite army God gave Judah victory because of their trust in him. Asa's prayer is a model for us - as we trust in God he is faithful to deliver v11.

***15:1-9* The LORD is with you when you are with him** We too will receive encouragement from the LORD - *if you seek him, he will be found by you v2*. Many of the people of the northern kingdom - Ephraim, Manasseh and Simeon migrated when they saw the blessing of God on Judah as a result of Asa's continuing reforms v9.

***15:10-19* Renewed Covenant** He brought all the people together to enter into a Covenant to seek the LORD with all their heart and soul v12. Yet high places of foreign worship remained in Israel v17.

***16:1-14* Collaboration with the world** Asa's faith weakened towards the end of his reign. When Judah was blockaded by Israel, their northern neighbor he called on the foreign king of Aram for help instead of relying on God - he paid a large tribune. He was reprimanded for this and imprisoned the prophet. We know that *the eyes of the Lord range throughout the earth to strengthen those whose hearts are fully committed to him v9*. God sees all things and looks for our response and commitment to him before acting. Asa turned from the LORD v10-12.

***17:1-19* Jehoshaphat** 873 BC – 25 years. He was a good king - in his early years his heart was devoted to the ways of the LORD v6. He sent teachers throughout Judah to instruct the people from the Book of the Law which had been neglected and the fear of the LORD came on the people - renewal will always break out in any age and group when the people of God turn devotedly to the Word of God v10; 1Kin 22:41-50.

***18:1-34* Self-dependence** As he was faithful to God Jehoshaphat became secure and prosperous. However this brought worldly alliances. He even married a daughter of Ahab the apostate king of Israel. We must not loose our primary dependence on the LORD.
Jehoshaphat joined with Ahab to recover Ramoth Gilead, a town taken by Aram. He requested that they inquire of the LORD before going to battle - *first seek the counsel of the LORD v4* - good advice but he did

not take it! The lying prophets of Israel gave a favorable word. Micaiah, the man of God contradicted them and was imprisoned.

18:28-34 Ahab was killed in the battle by a random arrow despite his subterfuge v29,33 as foretold by Elijah 1Kin 21:17-24. Jehoshaphat barely escaped with his life v31; 1Kin 22:29-33.

19:1-3 Jehoshaphat was rebuked for collaborating with Ahab.

19:4-11 He appointed fair judges and personally led Ephraim back to the LORD and keeping the Law.

20:1-30 **The Battle is the LORD'S** When Moab and Ammon from the south united to invade Judah Jehoshaphat called on God. His prayer was based on God's sovereignty and promises, on their own position of weakness and on their faith and trust in God – *our eyes are upon you v12*. God's response was prompt and to be expected – *do not be afraid or discouraged because - the battle is not yours but God's v15*. As they followed God's guidance with worship and praise they found deliverance, victory and reward. They returned joyfully and gave glory to God. This can be a pattern for our lives 2Kin 6:16,17.

20:31-37 Jehoshaphat was a good king but turned to worldly alliances in later years which did not receive God's blessing.

21:1-20 **Jehoram** 849 BC – 8 years. Jehoram was an evil king - he assassinated his six brothers to secure his position. His evil ways led to the rebellion of Edom and Libnah v8-11. Despite the evil the LORD maintained the royal line of David to fulfill his promise of the Messiah v7. The Philistines and Arabs raided Judah and carried off Jehoram's family. Elijah prophesied a disease which took his life v12-19; 2Kin 8:16-24.

22:1-9 **Ahaziah** 841 BC Ahaziah was evil and collaborated with Joram king of Israel. Both were killed by Jehu who was appointed by God to destroy the evil house of Ahab. Ahaziah's sons were executed in consequence of complicity with evil v7,8. Jehu became king of Israel 2Kin 9:1 to 10:36.

22:10-12 **Athaliah** mother of Ahaziah slaughtered the remaining royal family of Judah. This would have left no heir for David - however Jehosheba, daughter of Jehoram hid Joash youngest son of Ahaziah in the Temple while Athaliah ruled Judah for six years 2Kin 11:1-21.

23:1-21 **Joash** 836 BC – 40 years. When Joash was seven Jehoiada the priest led a coup to make Joash king. Athaliah was executed. A Covenant was made to be the LORD's people reinstating the Temple worship to the joy of the people v21.

***24:1-16* The Temple Repaired** Josiah undertook restoration of the Temple and fair administration of offerings 2Kin 12:1-21

***24:17-27* You have forsaken the LORD** When the priest died officials turned Joash away from God. They killed the messenger - Zechariah when he warned them *you will not prosper because you have forsaken the LORD v20,21*. Aram invaded Judah and Joash was assassinated.

***25:1-28* Amaziah** 797 BC – 29 years. Amaziah did right but not wholeheartedly. He embarked successfully in war against Edom and then against Israel but was defeated because he adopted the idols of Edom - he would not listen v15.

***26:1-23* Uzziah (Azariah)** 791 BC – 52 years. Uzziah did what was right and God gave him success v5. He became famous and powerful. But in later life pride led to his downfall – he treated the LORD with contempt - he sought to perform the priestly service and contracted leprosy v16.

***27:1-9* Jotham** 751 BC – 16 years. Jotham did what was right and succeeded because he walked steadfastly before God v6.

***28:1-27* Ahaz** 736 BC – 16 years. Ahaz did evil and was defeated by the kings of Aram and Israel. The surrounding nations of Philista and Edom attacked Judah. Ahaz sent to Assyria for help. Tiglath-Pileser III accepted tribute, conquered Damascus 732 BC, killed Rezin but did little to assist. Ahaz shut the Temple and turned further away from God.

***29:1-36* Hezekiah** 721 BC – 29 years. Hezekiah did right and began major reforms. He reopened the Temple, reinstated the Levites and cleared the sanctuary of idols. The people consecrated themselves and the Temple and renewed the Covenant with God. Sacrifices were made according to the Book of the Law and the services were re-established.

Fall of Samaria In the 4th year of the reign of Hezekiah 722 BC the northern capital of Samaria fell to Sennacherib king of Assyria and Israel was dispersed among the nations 2Kin 17:1-6.

***30:1-27* Passover** Hezekiah called people from throughout Judah and Israel to come to Jerusalem to celebrate the Passover, high point of the festive year which had long been neglected. They gave freely for the Temple services.

***31:1-21* So he prospered** The people were so encouraged they worked with the king throughout Judah to complete the reforms - *he sought his God and worked wholeheartedly - and so he prospered v21.*

32:1-9 Despite the reforms Sennacherib of Assyria invaded Judah 714 BC and captured the fortified cities. The fall of Lachish, some fifty km south west of Jerusalem is recorded on the wall of Sennacherib's palace 701 BC. Hezekiah fortified Jerusalem and secured the water supply to the city. The water tunnel inscribed by Hezekiah has been discovered. He encouraged the people to have faith in God's intention to save them - *there is a greater power with us than with him* v7,8. Jerusalem was spared because of that trust.

***32:9-23* Because you prayed to me** Sennacherib returned some time later but withdrew when the LORD intervened as a result of Hezekiah's prayer and as prophesied by Isaiah. He was subsequently assassinated v20,21; 2Kin 19:14-37; Is 37:21.

32:24-33 Hezekiah was granted an extension of life. These years were given *to test him and know everything that was in his heart* v31. They were not productive as he failed to give glory to God and bore an evil son 2Kin 20:1-21.

***33:1-20* Manasseh** 693 BC – 55 years. Manasseh did much evil and shed innocent blood so was taken prisoner to Assyria. When he repented he was returned and undertook reforms.

***33:21-25* Amon** 639 BC – 1 year. Amon did evil and was assassinated.

***34:1-13* Josiah** 638 BC – 31 years. Josiah was a good king from eight years old and introduced reforms. At twenty-six he began to purge the land by removing the places of idol worship and carried out repairs to the Temple.

***34:14-33* The Book of the Law** which had been forgotten was found in the Temple and applied - the Covenant was renewed. *Because your heart was responsive and you humbled yourself before God v27* - we will always obtain God's blessing when we return to the Word of God.

***35:1-19* Passover** Josiah celebrated the Passover, long neglected, with great enthusiasm among the people including many from Israel – a detailed description is given.

35:20-27 In 612 BC Nineveh, capital of Assyria fell to Babylon. Neco king of Egypt went to Carchemish near the Euphrates River. Josiah was killed in foolish conflict with Neco at the plain of Megiddo 609 BC Rev

16:16. Neco was subsequently defeated by Nebuchadnezzar, crown prince of Babylon 605 BC.

36:1-4 **Jehoahaz** 609 BC. Neco took tribune and deported Jehoahaz to Egypt

36:5-8 **Jehoiakim** 608 BC – 11 years. Nebuchadnezzar 605-562 BC attacked Jerusalem in 605 BC extracting tribute. He deported Jehoiakim and other nobles including Daniel to Babylon 2Kin 24:1,2.

36:9-10 **Jehoiachin** 598 BC. Nebuchadnezzar again besieged Jerusalem in 597 BC taking Jehoiachin and many officials including Ezekiel to Babylon.

Fall of Jerusalem 2Kin 24:18 to 25:21.

36:11-14 **Zedekiah** 597 BC – 11 years. Zedekiah rebelled against Nebuchadnezzar. The leaders of the priests and people became more unfaithful.

36:15-20 After a three year siege Nebuchadnezzar broke the walls of Jerusalem and set fire to the Temple 586 BC. The king and the officials were exiled to Babylon with only the poor left.

The reason for the fall of Israel and Judah was because the people had ignored and mocked God's messengers, despised his Word and scoffed at his warnings until the LORD was aroused against his people and there was no remedy v15,16.

36:21-23 **The Forecast Return from Exile** A remnant of the people will return from captivity after seventy years of Sabbath rests as prophesied by Jeremiah v 21; Jer 25:12 - compare with Ezr 1:1-3. The Books of Chronicles cover the record from Adam to the return giving encouragement to God's people.

Ezra - 'helps'

Introduction – The southern kingdom of Judah fell to Babylon in 586 BC and many of the people were taken into exile (also called 'the captivity'). Their sorrows are recorded in Ps 137.

Cyrus II, the Great of Persia 559-530 BC subdued Media in 549 BC and as king of Persia and Media conquered Babylon in 539 BC. The Books of Ezra and Nehemiah were originally one book describing events that followed when Cyrus gave the exiled people opportunity to return to their homeland in Jerusalem. The positive attitude of Cyrus was due to the tolerant policy of the Medes and Persians towards exiles. However it was no doubt encouraged by the good citizenship of the Jews during exile as instructed by Jeremiah Jer 29:1-32 and the prayers of God's people (Ezekiel, Daniel). Daniel who was in the king's court would have shown Cyrus the prophecies relating to him by Isaiah written some 150 before Is 45:1-7; Dan 6:28.

Most of the exiles were from the tribes of Judah, Benjamin and Levi but were collectively known as Jews from that time.

Author – Ezra, priest, scribe and reformer prepared this record of events in which he made a major contribution 7:1,10. He also likely coordinated the compiling and writing of the Books of Chronicles and may have been involved in establishing Synagogue worship during the captivity. He is believed to have led the group who formed the Old Testament Canon.

Period – The Books of Ezra and Nehemiah cover the return of the exiles which began in 538 BC and continued to 430 BC after Nehemiah made a second visit to Jerusalem Neh 13:6.

• **The first to return** in 538 BC were a group of some 50,000 under the leadership of Zerubbabel and Joshua. Zerubbabel was the master re-builder of the Temple and became governor of Judah Zec 4:9; Hag 2:2. Joshua was priest and later became high priest Zec 3:1. The Temple was completed and dedicated in 516 BC, the sixth year of Darius I 522–486 BC and seventy years after the fall of Jerusalem 586 BC as prophesied by Jeremiah Jer 25:12; 29:10. This was the subject of Daniel's prayer Dan 9:1-4. The people faced local opposition and were encouraged by the prophets Haggai and Zechariah. (The seventy years may be taken from Nebuchadnezzar's besiege of Jerusalem in 605 BC when Daniel began the Exile until 538 BC when the first people returned from Exile or from

586 BC when Jerusalem finally fell until the restoration of the Temple in 516 BC).

• **Ezra returned** to Jerusalem in 458 BC some 80 years after the first group and 58 years after the Temple dedication 7:8. He was the priest responsible for restoring formal Temple worship and reinstating the observance of the Law. - with him were some 1,800 priests, Levites and Temple servants.

• **Nehemiah returned** to Jerusalem as governor 13 years after Ezra's return to rebuild the walls and secure the city in 445 BC. He was recalled to Babylon 12 years later before returning to Jerusalem again Neh 13:6. These two Books of Ezra and Nehemiah together with the Books of Esther and Daniel provide the only Old Testament historical record of the Jewish people after the fall of Jerusalem.

Theme - The Return of the Remnant of Israel (Jews) to Jerusalem - this was a necessary step in God's plan for the coming of the Messiah for his kingdom to reach the whole world and

At the Right Time Ezra describes the return of the chosen people from captivity to a strategic position in the world at the time of the decline of the empires of the east - Assyria, Babylon, Persia, Egypt and the rise of the western empires of Greece and Rome. They re-established their worship and teaching of the Law in preparation for the coming of the Messiah Jesus Christ. God had kept his Covenant promise as he always does, just at the right time Gal 4:4.

Restoring Formal Worship The first priority of the returning Jews was to restore the Temple. After 22 years despite great opposition from the local people they succeeded in rededicating the Temple 6:13-18. Ezra arrived 58 years later with a group to educate the people in the observation of the formal worship and the Law as *written in the Book of Moses 6:18; 7:10.*

THE RETURN OF THE REMNANT FROM EXILE

1:1 Ezra identified the time of the return as the first year in Babylon of the reign of Cyrus king of Persia. It was in order to fulfill the Word of the LORD spoken by Jeremiah Jer 25:11-14. The fall of Babylon was also foretold by Isaiah 150 years before Is 44:28; 45:1-4. Daniel records that Cyrus, the Persian king appointed Darius, a Mede, as governor of Babylon while he continued his conquests. So he referred to the date of his vision as under Darius Dan 1:21; 9:1-2.

1:2-11 The decree was open to all who wished to return to their homeland. While the Jews had assimilated well into the land of exile many did return. Sheshbazzar prince of Judah was appointed governor of Jerusalem with charge of the treasury. He received some of the temple articles taken under Nebuchadnezzar to be returned 5:14.

2:1-70 A list is provided of 50,000 who went, all who were descendants of Israel.

Rebuilding the Temple.

3:1 The people first settled into their towns, establishing homes then when summoned reported to Jerusalem for duty.

3:2-6 **The Altar** Joshua the priest and Zerubbabel, who later became governor were in charge of construction. They began by building the altar so they could conduct offerings according to the Law of Moses v2. Then they celebrated the annual Feast of Tabernacles and other sacrifices as required.

3:7-13 **The Temple** They set to work to rebuilt the foundations of the Temple. When this was complete they celebrated with praise and thanksgiving. Some of the older people wept because they remembered the former glory that had been lost.

4:1-5 **Opposition to Rebuilding the Temple and Jerusalem** When the northern kingdom was conquered by Assyria the towns were settled with deported foreign people who intermarried with remaining Israelites, especially in Samaria. These people were now opposed to the rebuilding of Jerusalem. At first they sought to be involved but the Jews would not accept foreigners in the building of the Temple so the locals set out to frustrate the work. They made complaints to the Persian king and finally had the work stopped. This was possibly under Cambyses II 530-522 BC.

4:6-23 **Opposition to Rebuilding the City and Walls** Subsequently submissions were made to Xerxes (Ahasuerus) 486-465 BC, Esther's king and later to Artaxerxes 464-423 BC in opposition to the rebuilding of the city.

This accounts for the poor state of the work that caused Nehemiah to go to Jerusalem under the rule of Artaxerxes Neh 1:3.

4:24 The work on the Temple came to a standstill.

5:1-6:12 **The Prophets Haggai and Zechariah** ministered at the time of the rebuilding of the Temple and greatly encouraged the people to continue. They also foresaw the end time and the coming of Jesus Christ Hag 2:20-23; Zec 14:9. A further application was made to the new king

Darius I 522-486 BC who checked the records back to the time of Cyrus and agreed for the work on the Temple to be completed.

6:13-22 **Dedication of the Temple** The Temple was completed and dedicated in 516 BC in the sixth year of Darius 1. The people experienced great joy. This meant the LORD had forgiven them for their rebellion under the kings of Israel and Judah and was restoring the Temple worship. For eight days they celebrated the Passover and Feast of Unleavened Bread v19-22.

RETURN TO JERUSALEM

7:1-9 Ezra was led to seek permission from Artaxerxes in 458 BC to go to Jerusalem with some 2,000 of the descendents of the priests and Temple attendants. The opposition of the king to the building of the city and walls had changed 4:21. The journey took 4 months to travel the 700 km.

7:10 **The Need for Personal Preparation** Despite having been born in exile *Ezra had devoted himself to the study and observance of the Law of the LORD and to teaching its decrees and laws.* This confirms his capability to have coordinated the writing of the Books of Chronicles. He was now about to use his experience in the restored Temple and city. We must always do our best to train and be prepared to correctly handle the Word of God – we are God's workmen and we may not know what task the LORD is preparing us for 2Tim 2:15. Ezra was well qualified for the task at hand – restoring the observance of the Law and the formal Temple worship and recording the detailed history of the return from exile.

The study of the Word of God is vital for spiritual growth It is necessary to spend time in the reading and study of the Word of God on a regular basis in order for the significance of the Word to come to us – only then will we come to understand its importance in our daily life! Neh 8:1-8.

7:11-28 The king gave Ezra a letter which confirmed to the local people that permission was given to continue with the restoration of the Temple worship. Ezra praised God because he recognized this as God's hand v27.

8:1-14 The 1,700 registered family heads who returned with Ezra are listed.

***8:15-36* Confidence in the LORD** Ezra called a fast to seek the Lord's favor for a safe return – he was reluctant to ask further help from the king because of his expressed confidence in the LORD. On arrival in Jerusalem they gave thanks to God with sacrifices.

RESTORATION OF THE LAW OF THE LORD

9:1-15 Ezra began to address the conduct of the people in accordance with the Law of the LORD. These reforms continued over the next thirteen years and were not fully implemented until the arrival of Nehemiah when civil and religious leadership united for the good of the people Neh 8:1,9.

The desire for separation of Church and State comes from the intention of mankind to be independent from God and his ethical and moral laws. It is also the result of the failure of the Church to wholeheartedly embrace the teachings of God and Jesus Christ without pride and division and to present a unified message of salvation to the world Ps 133. This will be rectified in the eternal kingdom by the perfect prophet, priest and king Rev 11:15.

The people from the first group to return to Jerusalem had intermarried with the surrounding nations contrary to the Law. When Ezra discovered this he was appalled and confessed on behalf of the people.

10:1-44 They were convicted, acknowledging their sin and repented. They undertook the painful process of putting things right by separating from the foreign people. While this seems a harsh requirement it reminds us of the consequences of wrong decisions and the problems of restoration.

A Holy People We are also required to be a holy people - wholly committed to the ways and service of the LORD Mt 5:48.

Nehemiah

Introduction – This Book continues on from the Book of Ezra with the history of the exiles who returned from exile to Jerusalem - from Nehemiah's diary.

Author – Ezra, priest and scribe in Jerusalem at this time 12:26.

Period – The first visit of Nehemiah to Jerusalem to the completion of national reforms 445 to 430 BC. Artaxerxes 464-423 BC was son of Xerxes 486-465 BC who made Esther queen, a possible connection with Nehemiah, cupbearer in the royal court Est 2:17.

Theme – Rebuilding the defenses of Jerusalem and re-establishing Israel as a nation. This is an example of leadership and perseverance under severe opposition. It required the combined authority and commitment of the civil and religious leaders led by Nehemiah and Ezra to implement the reform.

Nehemiah's Focus - *I am doing a great work and will not be distracted 6:3.*

REBUILDING THE CITY OF JERUSALEM

1:1-3 In 445 BC the twentieth year of Artaxerxes king of Persia a party came from Jerusalem to Susa the capital of Persia where Nehemiah was cupbearer to the king, a position of great trust v11. The return of the exiles to Jerusalem had begun 94 years before and although the temple had been restored the city was unprotected and without organization.

1:4 When he heard of the poor state of the city Nehemiah turned to God in prayer – he sat down, wept, mourned and fasted, then he prayed Ezk 22:30.

1:5-11 **Importance of Prayer** This serves as a model for our communication with God -
*   praise and worship of God for his greatness and goodness
*   admission and confession of sin for the people
*   reminding God of his Word and promises Is 62:6,7
*   placing a request before God.

Nehemiah recognized his position of influence as cupbearer to the king and was ready to be used by God v11. He responded to the need of those in a position less fortunate than his own.

2:1-9 **Answer to Prayer** Artazerxes had initially opposed the rebuilding of Jerusalem Ezr 4:8,17. There was a change of heart when approached by Nehemiah after four months in answer to his prayer 2:1,6. The king agreed for Nehemiah to return to Jerusalem to complete the work and appointed him governor of the city 8:9. God enables those he calls to serve.

2:10 **Nehemiah's Return to Jerusalem** The appointment of a new governor did not please the locals. Nehemiah's return was in 445 BC some 13 years after Ezra. He worked with Ezra for the next 15 years.

2:11-16 **The Vision** - God put in his heart to do the work.

Get the facts - after arriving in Jerusalem Nehemiah set out by night to inspect the walls. A leader must always acquire firsthand detailed information, often gained in private if confronting opposition. Manage by facts, not hearsay or emotion v13.

2:17-20 **Communicating the Vision**
- *You see the trouble* - Identify with the people, describe the problem v17
- **What God has done** - Outline the plan and resources v18
- *Let us start* - Achieve the commitment of the people v18.

3:1-32 **Importance of Building Teams** The work was assigned to teams, a masterstroke of delegation. Forty teams were allocated work each in their own area of interest. Teams use collective skills, motivate each other and produce a greater return on their labor than the combined result of their individual efforts Ecc 4:9-12. Delegation empowers people and produces contribution and commitment - without it compliance and conformity. Areas of responsibility were clearly defined - everyone was involved.

4:1-3 **Remember who we are in Christ** As work progressed so did opposition, turning from ridicule to physical violence. We are God's people doing his work - the devil has no part in us.

4:4-23 **Good Strategic Plan** Nehemiah implemented a defense strategy -
- leading the people to pray to God for the work and for protection v4,9
- posting guards by day and night v9 - to allay fears and concerns so the workers could focus on the task v11-13
- addressing all problems as they arose and taking appropriate action v10-13
- reviewing progress firsthand to make decisions v14
- providing motivation and assurance from the top v14
- assigning tasks - half to work, half to stand guard v16

- those who could carried weapons while they worked v17
- remaining on alert at all times, ready for action v21,22

A trumpeter would signal emergency contingency plans v19.

5:1-19 People Focused Despite the demands of the project Nehemiah was quick to act to meet the needs of his people, especially when injustice occurred v7. He also instituted fair policies and worked on the wall himself - hands on management inspires involvement and understanding of the task. These actions gained the respect and commitment of all the people.

6:1-14 Task Focused As completion drew near the opposition increased. Subversive tactics were employed. Nehemiah would not be scared or deterred from the work God had given him, another sign of leadership.

6:15-19 Completion of the Wall was achieved after 52 days. The locals recognized that it was with the help of God.

7:1-73 Administration Authority for administration and security for the city was set up with a register of the inhabitants.

Renewal of Worship

8:1-18 Reading of the Word of God Now that the city was safe they turned to the service of God. The people assembled and Ezra brought out the Book of the Law of Moses. *He read it aloud from daybreak till noon – all the people listened attentively v3.* We need to listen to God's Word, daily.

The Levites then explained it making it clear to the people.

The people wept as they understood the meaning of the words of the Law v8,9. Nehemiah and Ezra told them not to weep but rejoice. This was a **sacred day** for the LORD had returned them to their homeland, made them secure and opened their hearts to the Word of God – *for the joy of the LORD is your strength v10.* The joy of the LORD will be our strength if we are open to the Word of God – *day after day v18.*

9:1-5 Response to God's Word The significance of God's Word came to the people. They recognized their sins, repented and confessed – in sackcloth and dust! A day was set aside for reading the Word, confession and worship.

9:5-38 Prayer of Worship and Commitment The people's prayer contained the following elements which are applicable in our own prayers–

- communication with God should always begin with praise based on who God is - his greatness and his faithfulness in keeping his promises v5
- acknowledging his holiness and recognizing our requirement to obey the Word of God - his ways and instructions v13
- confessing sins of the forefathers in not listening to God v16
- confession of one's own sins and repentance of them v37
- a binding agreement to follow the Law of God and his commands v38.

10:1-39 The agreement content and signatories were recorded.

Restoring the Nation

11:1 to 12:26 With the city secure many new residents arrived and were listed. A register of priestly families was established.

12:27-47 **Dedication of the Wall** A celebration was organized including activities used in the glory days of David and Solomon - *they offered great sacrifices, rejoicing because God had given them great joy v43.*

13:1-31 **Further Reforms** were introduced by Nehemiah in accord with the Law of the LORD in order to re-establish Israel as a nation under God.

Polytheistic worship was common in Judah and Israel in the time of the kings despite attempts at reforms. However there is no record of idol worship after the exile. Israel had become true to the one Eternal LORD God due to the lessons of the captivity and the reforms of Ezra and Nehemiah.

The Four Hundred Silent Years

The Old Testament historical record ends with the Book of Nehemiah 100 years after the return of the exiled Jews to Jerusalem.

The four hundred years from this time to the birth of Jesus are called the 'Silent Years' – a period when there was no prophetic Word from God.

Esther

Introduction – When Persia conquered Babylon in 539 BC Cyrus granted the exiled peoples the opportunity to return to their homelands Ez 1:1. Many decided to stay having established themselves in the country of exile.

The Persians embarked on world conquest. Darius I 522-486 BC was defeated by Greece at the battle of Marathon 490 BC. His son Xerxes (Ahasuerus) ruled Persia from 486–465 BC and mounted a major invasion of Greece by land and sea. Despite victory against the Spartans at Thermopylae Xerxes' fleet was destroyed in 480 BC at the battle of Salamis. It was in this period that Esther became queen.

Author – Mordecai, cousin of Esther, a Jewish exile and person of influence in the Persian court 2:7.

Period – During the reign of Xerxes after many of the Jewish exiles had returned to their homeland. Esther became queen in 479 BC. This was shortly before the return to Jerusalem of Ezra 458 BC and Nehemiah 445 BC.

Theme – God's providence and care are displayed in the placement of people and the outcomes of circumstances. He is always active without any conscious help from man, in every stage of history. He intervenes at the right time to fulfil his plan for mankind and chooses to use willing people. He is always behind the scenes in every aspect of your life.

God exerts influence over foreign godless people, nations and situations for the good of his people.

This series of events is of great importance to the Jewish people as an example of liberation from extermination.

There is no outward reference to God as is the case with many believers today and may have been prudent in a hostile society. But there is inner devotion and faith that produced responsibility and moral commitment in Mordecai and Esther. This contrasts with the godless conduct of the king and his associates.

There are examples of good and bad qualities in human nature –
• The king with his vanity, arrogance and vindictiveness
• Haman with his pride, resentment, hatred and obsession
• Esther with her loyalty, courage and commitment
• Mordecai with his care for Esther as an orphan, loyalty to Xerxes in reporting conspiracy and his service to his people.

The Persian Court

1:1-8 **The King's Excesses** Xerxes king of Persia ruled over the unified Medo-Persian Empire from the royal residence of Susa 300 km east of Babylon. There were 127 provinces compared with 120 in the time of Daniel 539 BC Dan 6:1.

The display of wealth and the seven day banquet (also recorded in secular history) occurred in 483 BC as Xerses prepared to avenge the defeat of his father by Greece in 490 BC.

The opulence of the celebration demonstrates the corrupt nature of unbridled power. Arrogance, self-centeredness and self-indulgence usually follow unconstrained power in the rise and fall of empires throughout history. The king's pride and ego led to the squandering of wealth accumulated at the expense of others for his pleasure and self promotion.

1:9-12 **The Queen Deposed** The revelry and alcohol led to a request for Vashti the queen to display her beauty before the male assembly, a request she refused. The king was furious as love for his queen turned to vindictiveness. Whatever other qualities Vashti may have had were ignored in his ruthless anger.

1:13-22 **Selective Counsel** The king surrounded himself with people who supported him, who told him what he wanted to hear. In an autocratic organization the people under the leader become more concerned about the leader's perception than about reality. They seek to appease the leader, to give the right answer, to make themselves secure and to promote their own interests. Unbiased advice requires fair and impartial leadership.

Domination is also a symptom of insecurity - if you have the skills trust God to use them to achieve the best result.

Male domination was at the core of the Persian system as is the case in most cultures today. Jesus liberated women and taught that we are all equal in the sight of God. Headship in the family is based on loving as Christ loved and submission to one another out of reverence for Christ Eph 5:21,28.

2:1-18 **A New Queen** The search for a replacement queen resulted in Esther becoming queen in 479 BC which was after the return of Xerxes from a crushing defeat at the battle of Salamis 480 BC v16. Mordecai, an exiled Jew, like Daniel and Nehemiah, rose to a position of importance in the court for he sat with the officials at the king's gate v19; 3:2. A cousin of Esther, he provided for her as an orphan. Esther underwent a twelve-month beauty treatment before being accepted by the king.

2:19-23 **The Conspiracy** The providence of God is evident in the uncovering of the earlier plan against the king and in Esther's position to report it. History records that Xerxes actually was assassinated eighteen years later in 465 BC in a similar plot by two of his disgruntled officers.

Privilege and Responsibility

3:1-15 **Abuse of Power** Haman received the high favor of the king being appointed as Chief Minister which should have produced gratitude and humility. Position brings responsibility to achieve the best contribution from the organization and the people. Instead of using his position of influence for the benefit of others Haman sought to bolster his ego by dominating those around him. Pride comes with position and must be dealt with. People in authority tend to reproduce after their kind – like Xerxes, like Haman!

As a faithful Jew Mordecai refused to bow before anyone but God as in the case of the fiery furnace and the lion's den Dan 3:16-18; 6:10. This enraged Haman who was himself an exile, an Agagite of the Amalekites, enemies of the Jews 3:1; Ex 17:8; 1Sam 15:3. This harbored a deeper resentment.

When he learned that Mordecai was a Jew he set out to exterminate all Jewish people. His personal bias and inflated vanity blinded him from seeing the potential in Mordecai which he should have utilized.

The indifference of the king to the proposed plan of genocide and confiscation of possessions showed no regard for justice or human life. Letters were sent throughout the Empire to implement the plan on a given day. While Haman sat down to drink the city of Susa was bewildered at this example of spiteful vengeance no doubt in fear of what could happen to them v15.

4:1-11 **An Action Plan** Persecution and adverse circumstances come to test our faith and our resourcefulness Jas 1:2-4. We can see them as impossible barriers and give up. Or we can recognize them as problems to be resolved, opportunities to be developed, steps to a greater goal – as did the two spies Nu 13:30; 14:6-8.

God always has a plan Mordecai began by seeking God in an outward expression of sorrow, a custom of the Jews. Esther came to learn of the crisis and was requested to petition the king.

Esther had been queen for 4 years 3:7. She had a position of status, comfort and security. Although she was an orphan she knew her privileged position was due to her God-given beauty, the care by Mordecai who had taken her as his own daughter, his promotion of her interests and her exalted status as queen. Yet she was now being asked to risk her life by coming before the king who insulated himself from his people. The king was not open to those who questioned his authority or judgment. Leaders must be open to the input and challenge of others to go beyond one's own comfort zone, address difficult issues and achieve the best result. We are not always right nor do we always have the best solution. Rather than curtail contribution the leader must ask questions to increase involvement and optimize the outcome.

4:12-17 Accepting Responsibility Mordecai was confident that God would provide deliverance for the Jewish people by some means. We must not think that our privileged position of comfort and security relieve us from being involved in ministry in the kingdom of God. We need to know our purpose in life. Esther had to decide if she was willing to be part of God's plan. Privilege always brings responsibility - status brings opportunity. We must each consider our own position and ask *who knows but that you have come to royal position for such a time as this? v14.* Our answer determines the degree to which we are available to be used in working out God's purposes in our time.

Esther faced her fear - *I will go to the king, even though it is against the law and if I perish, I perish v16* She knew she had little chance of success in her own ability and asked those involved to join her in fasting – with prayer and petition to God for guidance and courage. We tend to ask God to help us in what we are doing. Rather we must learn to be sensitive and responsive to what God is doing and wants to do in and through us! Ps 127:1; Zec 4:6.

5:1-8 The Plan Implemented Esther used her unique position as an opportunity. She knew the character of the king and Haman so she accepted the risk and stepped out in faith. She demonstrated trust in God - if we want to see the impossible we must move beyond the possible.

5:9-14 Consuming Passion Haman had received favor, position and influence yet he was consumed with hatred. His sense of achievement and fulfilment were overridden by ego, obsession and self-deception. Leaders must learn to keep personal feelings from distorting their reactions and decisions. Feelings must be controlled and used to achieve the objective, not allowed to cloud judgment and become vindictive or self-destructive. We harbor unresolved resentments, envy, bitterness, pride, self-importance and unforgiveness at the expense of wellbeing, peace of mind and sound judgment. Haman's family was party to the enmity.

6:1-14 **Loyalty Rewarded** It may have seemed that Mordecai's commitment to the king had been overlooked but God has his timing in recognizing and rewarding those who faithfully wait on him Mt 6:1-4. Again we see the sovereignty of God in the king's belated recognition of Mordecai. Haman's vanity began his downfall - before he could consider the warning of his family he was summoned to his ultimate fate v14.

7:1-10 **The Consequence of Hate** Esther's faith in God was vindicated by the events of the second banquet – *do not take vengeance but leave room for God's wrath Rom 12:19.* The king acted in her favor. There comes a time when we have to speak up for what we believe. Opportunities have been lost, injustice done, potential wasted, relationships broken, ministries destroyed because someone was afraid to speak the truth.

8:1 to 9:17 **God's People Delivered** The force of the second edict may seem harsh and unjust. However the first edict issued by Haman was designed to annihilate all Jews 3:8,9,13. While it was in force it was not to be implemented until the thirtieth day of the twelfth month 3:13. The law once issued could not be repealed according to the custom of the Medes and Persians 1:19; 8:5,8. It was therefore necessary to give the Jews the right to take up arms and defend themselves against the enactment of the first edict on the thirtieth day of the twelfth month 8:11,12. That they did not take plunder shows that the issue was one of survival 9:10. The edict had to be extended by one day.

9:18-32 **Feast of Purim** The Jews were successful in defending themselves. They rested on the following day with feasting, joy and thanksgiving to God v17. As a result of the deliverance the Feast of Purim was instituted as an annual celebration wherever Jews lived. Pur means 'lot' as cast by Haman to determine the day of vengeance 3:7.

Godly Leadership

10:1-3 **Faith Rewarded** Mordecai became Chief Minister with demonstrated ability 8:15; 9:3,4. He had proved his loyalty by reporting conspiracy to the king. In his official position he exercised integrity by not bowing to Haman. He took action against injustice to save his people.

He diligently served Xerxes, Esther, the Jewish people and the people of Persia.

Esther also showed leadership by recognizing her responsibility to her people. She used her privileged position for the good of Xerxes, her cousin and her people. That she continued to obey Mordecai speaks of the character of both Mordecai and Esther.

Many see the benefits of leadership as authority, power, privilege and prestige while ignoring the associated burdens of accountability, responsibility and duty. Leadership also involves humility and service Eph 4:1,2; Phil 2:1-5.

The Servant Leader – Jesus set the standard for leadership.

• He was tempted to choose the least costly way, to become a leader without suffering, pain, opposition or cost Mt 4:1-11

• In Gethsemane he accepted responsibility *'may this cup be taken from me, yet your will be done!' Mt 26:39.*

• He who would be great must be the servant Mt 20:25-28

• When he had served his disciples he told them - *now you know these things you will be blessed if you do them Jn 13:12-17*

• Understand that your success as a leader is the result of the effort and performance of your people - serve them accordingly.

Conclusion

Esther and Mordecai recognized that God had *determined the times set for them and the exact places they should live Acts 17:26.* He placed them in their positions of privilege for a purpose. We must see our position of privilege today and use it for the kingdom and others.

Judges & Kings Timeline

dates BC	1178	1140	1120 1110	1080 1070	1050 1040	1020 1010	990 970	930
Eli	b	j						
sons			j	d				
Ark Lost				d				
Samuel			b	j	d			
				End of Theocracy	⇧ ⇩ Beginning of Monarcy			
Saul				b	k			
David					b	k	d	
Solomon						k	b d	d
Temple							—	—
Kingdom Divided								

96

Significant Dates for Judges & Kings

date BC	born	judge	died	age
Eli	1178	1148	1080	98
Ark lost	1080	1000		
Samuel	1110	1080	1025	85

date BC	born	king	died	age
Saul	1080	1050	1010	70
David	1040	1010	970	70
Solomon	989	970	930	59
Temple				
commenced		996		
dedicated			959	

Basis for Calculation of Dates

	key date	reference
These are possible dates based on -		
Solomon was appointed king	970 BC	
Temple commenced in Solomon's 4th year	966	1Kin 6:1
Leaders were appointed at 30 years of age		2Sam 5:4
Leaders served 40 years (unless noted)	1Sam4:18	
Eli died at 98 (the Ark was lost).	1080	1Sam 4:15
Eli was judge for 40 years		1Sam 2:12
Samuel became judge at 30 when Eli died	1080	1Sam 7:2
Samuel's sons also served		1Sam 8:1
Request for a king in Samuel's 30th year	1050	1Sam 8:5
Saul became king – Samuel continued as priest	1050	1Sam 10:24
Samuel withdrew as Saul turned from God		1Sam 15:35
David was anointed at 10, Samuel was70		1Sam 16:13
Saul pursued David for 13 years		1Sam 27:1
Samuel died at 85 - David was 25		1Sam 25:
David became king over Judah at 30 years	1011	2Sam 5:4,5
David became king over all Israel at 37 years		1Chr 29:27
David brought the Ark to Jerusalem	1Chr 15:1	2Sam 6:1,2
David ruled for 40 years and died at 70 years	970 BC	1Chro29:27

Divided Kingdom of Judah

South			Kings	reign BC	yrs
Jerusalem			Rehoboam	930-914	17
344 years			Abijah	913-911	3
* 8 kings were good			Asa	* 910-870	41
12 kings were evil					
Prophets					
			Jehoshaphat	* 873-849	25
			Jehoram	849-842	8
			Ahaziah	841	
			Athaliah	841-836	6
			Joash	* 836-797	40
			Amaziah	* 797-768	29
			Azariah	* 791-740	52
			(Uzziah)		
	BC	yrs			
Isaiah	740-690	50	Jotham	* 751-736	16
Micah	740-700	40	Ahaz	736-721	16
			Hezekiah	* 721-693	29
Nahum	622-612	10	Manasseh	693-639	55
Zephaniah	625		Amon	639	
Jeremiah	626-580	46	Josiah	* 639-609	31
Joel	600		Jehoahaz	609	
Habakkuk	600		Jehoiakim	608-598	11
Obadiah	586		Jehoiachin	598	
Daniel	605-533	72	Zedekiah	597-586	11
Ezekiel	593-571	22	Fall of Judah 586		390
			(Jerusalem)		
CAPTIVITY			First captives	605	
RETURN			Fall of Babylon	539	
Haggai	520-516	4	First return	538	
Zechariah	520-516	4	Esther	480	
Malachi	430		Ezra	458-430	28
			Nehamiah	445-430	15
SILENT YEARS				400-0	
			Birth of the LORD JESUS CHRIST		

Divided Kingdom of Israel

Kings	reign BC	yrs	North		yrs
Jeroboam I	930-910	22	Samaria		
Nadab	910-909	2	208 years		
Bassha	909-886	24	All 19 kings were evil		
Elah	886-885	2			
Zimri	885				
Omri	885-874	12	**Prophets**	BC	
Ahab	874-853	22	Elijah	874-852	22
Ahaziah	853-852	2	Elisha	852-798	54
Joram	852-841	12			
Jehu	841-814	28			
Jehoahaz	814-798	17			
Jehoash	798-782	16	Jonah	760	
Jeroboam II	793-753	41	Amos	760-750	10
Zechariah	753-752		Hosea	757-722	35
Shallum	752				
Menahem	751-742	10			
Pekahiah	741-740	2			
Pekah	740-732	20			
Hosea	731-722	9			
Fall of Israel 722		241			
(Samaria)	Dispersed among the nations				
Fall of Assyria	612				
(Nineveh)					
Return from Babylon			After 70 years	605-538	
Temple dedicated	516				

Dates indicate start & end of reign or service.

The reigns of the kings are from the durations in the NIV.

SILENT YEARS				400-0	

Birth of the LORD JESUS CHRIST

99

BOOKS OF THE BIBLE
[39 + 27 = 66]

BOOKS OF THE OLD TESTAMENT
[39]

	HISTORY (17)	POETRY (5)	PROPHECY (17)	
LAW (5)	Genesis	Job	Isaiah	**MAJOR (5)**
Pentateuch	Exodus	Psalms	Jeremiah	
Books of Moses	Leviticus	Proverbs	Lamentations	
	Numbers	Ecclesiastes	Ezekiel	
	Deuteronomy	Solomon	Daniel	
HISTORY (12)	Joshua		Hosea	**MINOR (12)**
of Israel	Judges		Joel	
	Ruth		Amos	
	1 Samuel		Obadiah	
	2 Samuel		Jonah	
	1 Kings		Micah	
	2 Kings		Nahum	
	1 Chronicles		Habakkuk	
	2 Chronicles		Zephaniah	
	Ezra	Post Exile	Haggai	
	Nehemiah		Zechariah	
	Esther		Malachi	

BOOKS OF THE NEW TESTAMENT
[27]

	HISTORY (5)	LETTERS OF PAUL (13)	GENERAL LETTERS (9)	
GOSPELS (4)	Matthew	Romans	Hebrews	Unknown
	Mark	1 Corinthians	James	Other
	Luke	2 Corinthians	1 Peter	Apostles (7)
	John	Glatians	2 Peter	
Early Church (1)	Acts	Ephesians	1 John	
Luke		Philippians	2 John	
		Colossians	3 John	
		1 Thessalonians	Jude	
		2 Thessalonians	Revelation	John
		1 Timothy		
		2 Timothy		
		Titus		
		Philemon